AWAKENINGS

the Early Days

Ryan Phillips

AMBASSADOR INTERNATIONAL
GREENVILLE, SOUTH CAROLINA & BELFAST, NORTHERN IRELAND

www.ambassador-international.com

Awakenings

ISBN: 978-1-62020-831-1
eISBN: 978-1-62020-837-3

Cover Design & Typesetting by Hannah Nichols
Ebook Conversion by Anna Riebe Raats

AMBASSADOR INTERNATIONAL
Emerald House
411 University Ridge, Suite B14
Greenville, SC 29601, USA
www.ambassador-international.com

AMBASSADOR BOOKS
The Mount
2 Woodstock Link
Belfast, BT6 8DD, Northern Ireland, UK
www.ambassadormedia.co.uk

The colophon is a trademark of Ambassador, a Christian publishing company.

I WAS TWENTY-SEVEN YEARS OLD when I moved to the Big Island of Hawaii. At that point in my life, I had seen and experienced a few things. I was born in New York City and spent seven years in Connecticut as a child. At the age of nine, my father and mother became missionaries to Spain, and we lived there for six years. Upon returning to Connecticut, I hardened my heart to God. I spent eight years away from Him. In that time, I earned a college degree and obtained a high-paying job in New York City. I experienced the depths of sin: lust, greed, and drunkenness in the city that never sleeps. I fell in love—or what I thought was love—and had my heart broken. I found myself crying often and couldn't understand why. I began writing dark poetry and drinking more.

One night, I locked myself in my room and started to read the book of Proverbs. Revelation and sorrow followed. I decided to move back home to Connecticut and commute to New York City. Mom and Dad began to give me books to read during my hour-and-a-half commute to New York City on the train. I read John Elderidge's *Wild at Heart* and several other books. I decided to quit my job and go hike the Appalachian Trail. I spent three amazing months in the wilderness of Georgia, Tennessee, Virginia, and West Virginia. I felt God's presence out there and started to read parts of the Word.

After this, I spent four years working carpentry in Connecticut. I met a man named Jim Braun at work. In the middle of winter, we were installing cedar shingles on a roof in New York State. I slipped and shot a nail into my leg just above my knee cap. Jim came to the rescue and quickly pulled the nail out with a pair of lineman pliers. A few months later,

Jim invited me to Hawaii to help him and his wife, Joyce, build a retirement home in Laupahoehoe, Hawaii.

The first three months on the island, God blessed me with revelation in the early morning hours as I sat in a field overlooking the ocean and began to listen and read the Word. I wondered why it had taken me so long to get to this place. The peace, beauty, and joy of daily life with God is indescribable. I thank and praise Him for bringing me to the edge and rescuing me from the grasp of Satan.

The following is a collection of words that I wrote during my first season on the East Coast of the Big Island of Hawaii. I am grateful to Thomas and Leslie Jordan, who encouraged me to write and share with others. I am also grateful to Jane Testa who gave me a place to stay last year and time to type these devotionals out from the original handwritten journal I wrote in 2008.

SOLDIER

ALL THE MEN IN MY family have been military men. My father was in the navy. My brother was in the marines. My uncle on my mother's side was a marine. Both my uncles on my father's side are marines. I felt that I was falling short in this area and that I should serve. Then God revealed to me, "You are a member of My family, and I will make you a soldier in My army." Ephesians 6:13-17 says:

> Therefore take up the whole armor of God, that you may be able to withstand in the evil day, and having done all, to stand. Stand therefore, having girded your waist with truth, having put on the breastplate of righteousness, and having shod your feet with the preparation of the gospel of peace; above all, taking the shield of faith with which you will be able to quench all the fiery darts of the wicked one. And take the helmet of salvation, and the sword of the Spirit, which is the word of God.

HIS WAYS

Solid are His Ways.

They break through the hardest of hearts

And lift up the depressed soul.

He can transform the vilest of mankind.

Never doubt His power, for doubt renders you powerless.

Faith can leave you speechless,

Unable to talk or walk on your own, but living in His Spirit

Like an Arctic tern flying to its home.

"Let everything that has breath praise the Lord. Praise
the Lord!"

-Psalm 150:6

WILLING

MANY OF US PROCLAIM THAT we follow God and His Son, Jesus. We proclaim it with our mouths. We praise Him with our lips. We say we are willing to do whatever He tells us. How uncomfortable are you willing to be? How embarrassed? How about humiliated, mocked, scourged, and put to death? *Will* is such a small word, yet it controls the majority of what we do. Jesus said, "The spirit indeed *is* willing, but the flesh *is* weak" (Matt. 26:41). We are all weak and fall short often. God has chosen the weak as vessels to show His strength.

> "For what I am doing, I do not understand. For what I will to do, that I do not practice; but what I hate, that I do" (Rom. 7:15).

Remember you are saved by grace! Live in the Spirit!

COMPLAINTS

A COMPLAINT IS THE ANTITHESIS of faith. If we truly believe that God is in control, we would never complain. Do you complain about your life? Has God not delivered you from the oppression you once lived under? Was the Exodus not powerful and great? How quickly we forget, and complaining creeps in. Accept the burdens He has placed on you because they are meant to refine you. When you are able to walk through difficulties without complaint, others will be blessed and drawn to God.

> "Come to Me, all *you* who labor and are heavy laden, and I will give you rest. Take My yoke upon you and learn from Me, for I am gentle and lowly in heart, and you will find rest for your souls. For My yoke is easy and My burden is light" (Matt. 11:28-30).

DRAWING

WHICH WELL ARE YOU DRAWING from—the eternal well of Jesus or the empty well of the world? Do you spend two hours watching a captivating movie and only ten minutes listening to God? Are you more interested in the next meal than the nourishment of His Word? Do you wonder where God is in your life? If you spend more time drawing from the worldly pleasures than you do devouring God's Word, then you cannot expect to see lasting fruit in your life.

> "Therefore submit to God. Resist the devil and he will flee from you. Draw near to God and He will draw near to you. Cleanse *your* hands, *you* sinners; and purify *your* hearts, *you* double-minded. Lament and mourn and weep! Let your laughter be turned to mourning and *your* joy to gloom. Humble yourself in the sight of the Lord, and He will lift you up" (Jas. 4:7-10).

MERE TRADITIONS: THE NAKED TRUTH

BE CAREFUL OF MAKING ANY activity a routine or a tradition. The danger is that you will begin to favor that thing over the will of God. When Jesus walked on the earth, He rebuked the Pharisees and scribes for their traditions. *"All too* well you reject the commandment of God, that you may keep your tradition" (Mk. 7:9). If you are a creature of habits and routines, this will be difficult for you, but ask God to rid you of any routines that are not from Him. When He does, you will realize that you are able to walk through all obstacles put in your way along this journey. When Job was informed that all his sons and daughters had been killed in the same day, he fell to the ground and worshipped.

> "Naked I came from my mother's womb, And naked shall I return there. The Lord gave, and the Lord has taken away; Blessed be the name of the Lord" (Job 1:21).

GIANTS & GRASSHOPPERS

WE ALL HAVE GIANTS THAT oppose God in our lives. Obstacles that seem impossible. Circumstances that are too difficult for us. God instructed Moses to send out the leaders of the tribes of Israel to spy on the land of Canaan. This was the land that God had promised the Israelites. Out of twelve leaders, only two wanted to take the land. The others responded, "There we saw the giants . . . and we were like grasshoppers in our own sight, and so we were in their sight" (Num. 13:33). Fear caused the people to rebel. They saw themselves as grasshoppers instead of as God's people. If you see yourself as small and insignificant, others will see you as such. Remember that alone we are defeated, but through Him, we are more powerful than any giant. David slew the giant Goliath in the Valley of Elah because he knew in his heart that God was with him. If God is with us, who can stand against us? Put your faith in God, conquer your fears, and battle the giants!

DIVIDE AND CONQUER

SATAN'S WAY OF HINDERING GOD'S work in a church body is simply to create division amongst brothers and sisters. He will implant thoughts of negativity, pessimism, and opposition in the minds of many. Arguments will arise over petty details. Certain people will agree with one another against other members. When these situations arise, make sure you submit them to God so that you don't become an instrument for Satan's work. Does the outside world see a church of unity and love or a divided and defeated people? Guard your mind from the enemy of your soul.

> "But avoid foolish disputes, genealogies, contentions, and strivings about the law; for they are unprofitable and useless. Reject a divisive man after the first and second admonition, knowing that such a person is warped and sinning, being self-condemned" (Titus 3:9-11).

HIS WORKMANSHIP

EVERY BUILDING HAS ONE STARTING point from which all other points are drawn from. This is the foundation. Jesus needs to be our starting point. We take all measurements from there. If we misread Jesus, we end up with a poorly built house. From the foundation to the frame to the finishing touches, all are affected by the foundation. As a carpenter, I have seen how something done wrong during framing makes the finishing touches very difficult. As God completes His good work in us, we need to be sure we have heard and interpreted His instructions accurately. Make sure to correct errors when they happen because it is difficult to go back later. Do not reject the building instructions of God as the world does.

> "The stone *which* the builders rejected Has become
> the chief cornerstone. This was the Lord's doing; It
> *is* marvelous in our eyes" (Psa. 118:22-23).

ZEAL AND RAGE

WEBSTER'S DICTIONARY DEFINES ZEAL AS "eagerness and ardent interest in pursuit of something." In the Bible, we see zeal side by side with a sorrowful rage. In a rage, the son of a priest slays a fellow Israelite, who was committing harlotry with a foreign woman. God responds by blessing him, saying: " . . . behold, I give to him My covenant of peace; and it shall be to him and his descendants after him a covenant of an everlasting priesthood, because he was zealous for his God, and made atonement for the children of Israel" (Num. 25:12-13).

Another Son raged against the church in the New Testament. This was the Son of the Most High God.

> When He had made a whip of cords, He drove them all out of the temple, with the sheep and the oxen, and poured out the changers' money and over-turned the tables. And He said to those who sold doves, "Take these things away! Do not make My Father's house a house of merchandise!" Then His disciples remembered that it was written, "Zeal for Your house has eaten Me up" (Jn. 2:15-17).

Jesus would bring atonement, not only to the Israelite people but also to all mankind, who put their faith in Him.

> "The Lord shall go forth like a mighty man; He shall stir up *His* zeal like a man of war. He shall cry out, yes, shout aloud; He shall prevail against His enemies" (Isa. 42:13).

INTERCESSION

WE ADMIRE HEROISM IN OUR society—people who sacrifice themselves for others. A soldier lays down his life to save his fellow soldiers; a man offers his life in place of a woman or child. What about the extreme: laying down your life for wicked people? Moses made intercession for the Israelites constantly. Several times God was going to destroy the Israelites for their wickedness, but Moses interceded:

> "Thus I prostrated myself before the Lord; forty days and forty nights I kept prostrating myself, because the Lord had said He would destroy you" (Deut. 9:25).

Moses gave his life for these people, even though they still rebelled repeatedly. Most of the priests in the Old Testament, who made intercession for the people, would die at an appointed time and place. Jesus, however, represents a new covenant:

> "By so much more Jesus has become a surety of a better covenant. Also there were many priests, because they were prevented by death from continuing. But He, because He continues forever, has an unchangeable priesthood. Therefore He is also able to save to the uttermost those who came to God through Him, since He always live to make intercession for them" (Heb. 7:22-25).

THE LIVING WORD

MOST THINGS IN LIFE EXPIRE or become outdated. New technology replaces inferior technology; advances in medicine change doctors' advice; and scientific discoveries change our view of the world. We no longer believe the earth to be flat but know it to be round. The prophet Isaiah declared these words when people believed the earth to be flat: "It is He who sits above the circle of the earth . . . " (Isa. 40:22).

How is it that the things written in the Bible still speak to us today? Is it because the soul of man has remained the same throughout many generations? We know that God hasn't changed. He is the same yesterday, today, and forever! The truth is, despite all the worldly changes, people still struggle with the same things. Our only hope is in the Living Word.

> "For the Word of God *is* living and powerful, and sharper than any two-edged sword, piercing even to the division of soul and spirit, and of joints and marrow, and is a discerner of the thoughts and intents of the heart" (Heb. 4:12).

PURE RELIGION AND JUSTICE

RELIGION HAS A LEGALISTIC SOUND to it. We prefer to say we have a relationship with our God. Religious people are rigid and strict. Don't do this, and you cannot do that. Religion was meant to be pure. One definition of religion from *Webster's Dictionary* is "a cause, principle, or system of beliefs held to with ardor and faith." The Greek word for religion is *threskeia* and means "ceremonial observance." The root of this word is *threskos,* which means "ceremonious in worship." Pure religion is defined differently by James:

> "Pure and undefiled religion before God and the Father is this: to visit orphans and widows in their trouble, *and* to keep oneself unspotted from the world" (Jas. 1:27).

This was not a new concept of the New Covenant. Moses instructed Israel: "You shall rejoice before the Lord your God, you and your son and your daughter, your male servant and your female servant, the Levite who *is* within your gates, the stranger and the fatherless and the widow who *are* among you, at the place where the Lord your God chooses to make His name abide" (Deut. 16:11).

Pure religion is to rejoice before the Lord and to love strangers, widows, orphans, and anyone who is within the realm of where God has placed you. We are also called to do justice:

> "You shall not pervert justice due to the stranger or the fatherless, nor take a widow's garment as a pledge" (Deut. 24:17).

SECRET SEARCHING

HUMANS ARE ALWAYS QUESTIONING. WHY this or why that? We want to know the reasons for everything. We are upset when we don't get answers. Our educational system encourages young minds to question everything, including God. When we don't receive explanations, we decide that the thing we don't understand is false. If you don't understand how the mechanics of your car work, does that mean the car ceases to work or be reliable? Of course not! Sometimes, faith is required to accept the secret things and search out the revealed truths from God.

> "The secret *things belong* to the Lord our God, but those *things which are* revealed *belong* to us and to our children forever, that *we* may do all the words of this law" (Deut. 29:29).

DRUNKEN PEACE

HIS PEACE IS EVERLASTING. IT is not fleeting like worldly peace. When we drink of His waters, we become drunk with His peace. Circumstances don't matter. Time doesn't matter. This life doesn't matter. The world will tell you to focus on yourself. Self-esteem and pride are of high importance to mankind. God despises this belief:

> "So that there may not be among you man or woman or family or tribe, whose heart turns away today from the Lord our God, to go *and* serve the gods of these nations, and that there may not be among you a root bearing bitterness or wormwood; and so it may not happen, when he hears the words of this curse, that he blesses himself in his heart, saying, 'I shall have peace , even though I follow the dictates of my heart'—as though the drunkard could be included with the sober" (Deut. 29:18-19).

If you are following after your own heart, you will never achieve the peace that surpasses understanding. A drunkard is never at peace in his mind, body, or soul—even if he thinks he is.

> "On the last day, that great day of the feast, Jesus stood and cried out, saying, 'If anyone thirsts, let him come to Me and drink. He who believes in Me, as the Scripture has said, out of his heart will flow rivers of living water" (Jn. 7:37-38).

GARBAGE OR GOLD

DOES THE LORD RECEIVE THE best of all you have, or do you reserve for Him the things you consider garbage? It is obvious where God ranks in your life by what you turn over to Him. God doesn't have any need for your gold, but are you willing to give it? He can transform garbage into gold the same way Jesus turned water into wine. Abraham was ready to sacrifice Isaac, and God did sacrifice Jesus. Giving up our garbage makes us feel better about ourselves, but giving up the things we love is painful. God is faithful when we sincerely love Him.

> "But take careful heed to do the commandment and the law which Moses the servant of the Lord commanded you, to love the Lord your God, to walk in all His ways, to keep His commandments, to hold fast to Him, and to serve Him with all your heart and with all your soul" (Josh. 22:5).

GOD IS LOVE

TO LOVE GOD IS TO pour out His love on others. We cannot truly love without taking on the life of God's Son, Jesus, and receiving the Holy Spirit. Genuine love comes from the Trinity, and any other love has some basis in selfishness. Our calling in this life is to reflect the love that God has poured into our lives. The problem is that we only experience this love when we abandon ourselves for Him. We have to live a life filled with Jesus's perspective.

> "In this the love of God was manifested toward us, that God has sent His only begotten Son into the world, that we might live through Him" (1 Jn. 4:9).

We cannot love God while hating another human being. Scripture explains how this is impossible.

> "If someone says, 'I love God,' and hates his brother, he is a liar; for he who does not love his brother whom he has seen, how can he love God whom he has not seen" (1 Jn. 4:20).

CONSTANT HUMILITY

IT IS EASY TO PORTRAY humility in any given moment. To be constantly humble is what we struggle with. Gideon is a good example. God used him to deliver the Midianites into the hands of Israel. When Gideon delivered this victory to the Israelites, they requested that Gideon and his family rule over them. These are a people who had previously turned away from God to worship Baal.

> "But Gideon said to them, 'I will not rule over you, nor shall my son rule over you; the Lord shall rule over you'" (Judg. 8:23).

In Gideon's next breath, he asks the people for the earrings from their plunder, and he creates an idol of worship with them. "And all Israel played the harlot with it there. It became a snare to Gideon and his house" (Judg. 8:27). Gideon had declared that the Lord would rule over them, but he makes an idol. He has contradicted himself and immediately steps out in his own desires. Be careful of anyone who sings your praises—it can make you lose your humility and favor with God. God loves a humble heart.

> "Surely He scorns the scornful, But gives grace to the humble" (Prov. 3:34).

BARRENNESS AND FRUITFULNESS

THE BIBLE IS FULL OF stories of people who experience both being barren and fruitful. God loves to transform the barren into fruitful and vice versa. In Genesis alone, we see several examples of barren women giving birth: Sarah (16:1), Rebekah (25:21), and Leah and Rachel (29:31). When God met with Moses on Mount Sinai and gave Moses the law, He promised:

> "No one shall suffer miscarriage or be barren in your land; I will fulfill the number of your days" (Exod. 23:26).

> "This promise was secured by the obedience of the people and the agreement that they would serve the Lord alone. The people broke this agreement over and over. Samson was born to a barren woman" (Judg. 13:3).

I believe the psalmist describes this best:

> "He turns rivers into a wilderness, And the watersprings into dry ground; A fruitful land into barrenness, For the wickedness of those who dwell in it. He turns a wilderness into pools of water, And dry land into watersprings" (Psa. 107:33-35).

The entire Psalm exhibits God's power to transform. Look back at the barrenness of your own life and remember how He continues to transform you daily. Look at the Gospel of Luke and how John the Baptist was born to a barren woman, and Jesus was born to a virgin.

FAMILY MATTERS

IT IS IMPORTANT TO SUPPORT our families, especially when they have been beaten up or discouraged by the circumstances of their lives. Love is not just a word; it involves action to become genuine. It requires putting aside our own needs and desires to serve others.

In the Bible, we see Ruth doing this with her mother-in-law, Naomi. Naomi had lost her husband and two sons. Her daughters-in-law were all she had left of her family, and she decided to cut them loose. When things go bad for us, we tend to want to be alone. Ruth recognized this and declared to Naomi:

> " . . . Entreat me not to leave you, *Or to* turn back from following after you; For wherever you go, I will go; and wherever you lodge, I will lodge; Your people *shall be* my people, And your God, my God" (Ruth 1:16).

Naomi had become bitter toward God and wanted to let go of everything. Ruth refused to let her continue being bitter. She took action and worked hard to support Naomi. Ruth is our example of how to deal with family. God is good and has placed you in a family to bring Him glory.

HANNAH'S PRAYER

HANNAH GRIEVED HER BARRENNESS. SHE cried out to the Lord to give her a male child and made a vow to give that child back to the Lord. So, Hannah gave birth to Samuel.

Hannah's prayer in chapter two of First Samuel describes the Almighty power of God and the failure of human power. We rarely cry out to God in desperation anymore because we have filled ourselves with worldly things. Food, sex, and entertainment have consumed us. We are quick to speak when we should be listening. Arrogance reigns in our hearts, even though we know our knowledge is empty. Our faith is one that requires testing to be real.

> "Those who were full have hired themselves out for bread, And the hungry have ceased *to hunger*. Even the barren has borne seven, And she who has many children has become feeble" (1 Sam. 2:5).

As you grow in the Lord, you need to be aware of how powerful He is to change any circumstance. Cry out to Him, and commit yourself to Him as Hannah did.

TRUTH

THE TRUTH SHALL SET YOU free. Everyone has heard this saying at least once. Yet, we live in a world where the truth is hidden from us, and we are told that we need to find truth for ourselves. Today, everyone defines truth for themselves. The problem is there can only be one truth, and everything else is automatically a lie. A slight variation of the truth can be even more harmful to us than an obvious lie. Watch carefully for the perversion of the truth. The truest words ever spoken:

> "Jesus said to him, 'I am the way, the truth, and the life. No one comes to the Father except through Me'" (Jn. 14:6).

Never alter the truth or hide the truth from each other because this is a sin against God. It separates you from Him. In the Old Testament, we see how God would punish those who hid the truth—from Adam and Eve in Genesis all the way through the book of Malachi. God spoke to Samuel when he was a little boy, telling him that He would destroy Eli and his sons for their iniquity. Eli had served Israel as judge for forty years. God chose a boy to deliver His message to Eli. Samuel spoke the truth and hid nothing from Eli. Do you have the courage to speak the truth, even when it is condemning those you love? Read First Samuel three.

TURNING ASIDE

WE ARE SO QUICK TO forget the things that God has done for us. Like horses with blinders on, we only see what is directly ahead of us. Unable to see what is in the surroundings or behind us, we make decisions based on our limited vision. We desire the material things that others have. Israel desired a human king to reign over them. They were not satisfied to be led by God, Who they could not see. Humans are willing to suffer all kinds of misery pursuing something we can see rather than having faith in the unseen. God granted Israel's wish to have a king. Samuel anointed Saul to rule over them:

> "And when you saw that Nahash king of the Ammonites came against you, you said to me, 'No, but a king shall reign over us,' when the Lord your God *was* your king" (1 Sam. 12:12).

In our stubbornness, we demand things. God often grants our wishes to show us how empty they are. If you are pursuing wealth, He will show you a wealthy person who is unsatisfied. If you are pursuing a partner, He will show you the struggles or heartache that come with trying to find fulfillment in anyone but Him. Whatever it is that you are pursuing will lead you to emptiness, unless God is leading you.

> "And do not turn aside; for *then you would go* after empty things which cannot profit or deliver, for they *are* nothing" (1 Sam. 12:21).

HEART CONDITION

THE PHRASE "HEART CONDITION" HAS a negative connotation to it. We automatically think of a heart attack or high blood pressure. God looks at our hearts first and foremost—not for high blood pressure, but to see our motive for doing things. We have reasons for all the things we do. They are often not righteous or pure reasons. We question God as to why we don't find favor from Him, yet we do little to change our heart condition.

> "The Lord has sought for Himself a man after His own heart . . . " (1 Sam. 13:14b).

King David was a man after God's heart. Despite his sins, he found favor with God. We need to start seeking after God's heart in order to transform our own. It is only when we embrace God's heart that we will see Him amongst us.

> "Blessed *are* the pure in heart, For they shall see God" (Matt. 5:8).

SPECIFIC OBEDIENCE

WE CAN BELIEVE THAT WE were obedient in a situation when, in fact, we did not do everything we were asked to do. It is important that we know God's general will for our lives and that we obey His commandments.

Saul, the first king of Israel, was guilty of disobedience. He was told by Samuel that God wanted him to utterly destroy the Amalekites. However, Saul spared the Amalekite king his life and also kept the best of the livestock and anything that was good. When Samuel confronted Saul, he heard excuses.

> "But the people took of the plunder, sheep and oxen, the best of the things which should have been utterly destroyed, to sacrifice to the Lord your God in Gilgal" (1 Sam. 15:21).

Saul does two things: he blames others, and he makes it seem like he was doing this for God. God does not need us to do things for Him; He wants us to be obedient.

> "So Samuel said: 'Has the Lord *as great* delight in burnt offerings and sacrifices, As in obeying the voice of the LORD? Behold, to obey is better than sacrifice, *And* to heed than the fat of rams" (1 Sam. 15:22).

I hear many people say we are living in the age of grace. The New Testament is the New Covenant. This is truth, but God still desires us to walk in obedience to His voice. God is the same yesterday, today, and forever.

JEALOUSY

JEALOUSY IS THE OUTCOME OF selfishness. When we begin to want what others have, we fall into this trap. We want good things to happen to us; but when God's blessings are poured out on another, we begin to feel jealous. Sometimes, the blessings God has poured out on others are also a blessing to us, but jealousy has blinded us to that fact. Only the Spirit of the Lord can combat jealousy. The Spirit of the Lord rested heavily on David when he dealt with Saul's jealousy. David returned hatred with love, deceitfulness with honesty, and cowardice with courage.

> "Now Saul was afraid of David, because the Lord was with him, but had departed from Saul" (1 Sam. 18:12).

You see, it is possible to fight and overcome men, but it is impossible to fight the Spirit of the Lord. The outcome of jealousy is always negative. If you react to jealousy with revenge, you lose the battle. Let God guide you and impart this wisdom to you. This is the only way to combat jealousy in your own life and the lives of others.

> "And David behaved wisely in all his ways, and the Lord *was* with him" (1 Sam. 18:14).

IRRESISTIBLE SPIRIT

THE SPIRIT OF GOD IS irresistible. It has the power to stop any man. In the Bible, we see men of great worldly power being stopped in an instant and becoming overcome by the Spirit. This is the supernatural way God intervenes on behalf of His followers. David was able to escape the hand of Saul. Saul had pursued David to Ramah to kill him, but the Spirit of God overcame Saul:

> "Then the Spirit of God was upon him also, and he went on and prophesied until he came to Naoioth in Ramah. And he also stripped off his clothes and prophesied before Samuel in like manner, and lay down naked all that day and all that night. Therefore they say, 'Is Saul also among the prophets'" (1 Sam. 19:23-24).

Saul of the New Testament also persecuted God's people. He persecuted the disciples and pursued after them until the Spirit of God overcame him on the road to Damascus.

> "As he journeyed he came near Damascus, and suddenly a light shone around him from heaven. Then he fell to the ground, and heard a voice saying to him, 'Saul, Saul, why are you persecuting Me'" (Acts 9:3-4).

The Spirit of God can overcome anyone. It changed Saul into Paul, who became one of the most powerful Christians in the New Testament.

OVERCOMING EVIL

GOD'S RIGHTEOUSNESS IS FOUND IN doing good to others, even when they are not good to us. We must always turn the other cheek. When Saul tried to kill David, David was exceedingly good to Saul. David could have killed Saul in the caves of En Gedi, but he didn't. David proved to Saul that he would never raise his hand against him. Saul responded, "You are more righteous than I; for you have rewarded me with good, whereas I have rewarded you with evil" (1 Sam. 24:17b).

You see, when we return evil for evil, we end up losing the battle. An eye for an eye leaves us both blind. Good is the only thing that triumphs over evil. This is the story Jesus conveyed at the cross—to love those who hated Him, even to the point of death.

> "Do not be overcome by evil, but overcome evil with
> good" (Rom. 12:21).

Evil has no power against Love.

WEEPING WARRIORS

TODAY, THE WORLD VIEWS MEN who cry or weep as weak. As a generation, we have lost our compassion for others. Our tears come from intense pain or self-pity. God desires a compassionate people, not an indifferent crowd. Weeping should be the first reaction of the warrior, followed by action. David and his men returned to their city to find it burned and their families taken.

> "Then David and the people who *were* with him lifted up their voices and wept, until they had no more power to weep" (1 Sam. 30:4).

Injustice, abuse, violence, and all other forms of evil offend God, and they should offend us—at least, to the point of tears. Ezekiel was given revelation and visions from God. God revealed the abominations taking place within the city of Jerusalem and the nation of Israel. In Ezekiel 9:1, the Lord instructs "those who have charge over the city" to slay the wicked but spare those who cry over the abominations being done.

> "And the Lord said to him, 'Go through the midst of the city, through the midst of Jerusalem, and put a mark on the foreheads of the men who sigh and cry over all the abominations that are done within it" (Ezek. 9:4).

Weeping is a powerful tool for a warrior in God's army.

SINCERE WORSHIP

WHAT DOES WORSHIP LOOK LIKE when it is sincere? When we are truly worshipping, the Holy Spirit comes over us in a powerful way. We no longer care about how we appear to others. Free from any regimented or designed style, there begins a natural flow of the Spirit within us. To the skeptical observer, this may appear to be wild behavior, but this observer is observing and not worshipping. Letting go of your insecurity is necessary to truly worship.

> "Then David danced before the Lord with all *his* might" (2 Sam. 6:14).

Michal, Saul's daughter, observed David, "and she despised him in her heart" (2 Sam. 6:16b). She confronted David later, saying, "How glorious was the king of Israel today in the eyes of the maids of his servants, as one of the base fellows shamelessly uncovers himself" (2 Sam. 6:20). David replied:

> "And I will be even more undignified than this, and will be humble in my own sight" (2 Sam. 6:22a).

God desires a people who will worship Him with everything they have. Jesus explained to the woman at the well:

> "But the hour is coming, and now is, when the true worshipers will worship the Father in spirit and truth; for the Father is seeking such to worship Him" (Jn. 4:23).

SPIRALING SIN

SIN CAN START FROM WHAT seems to be something harmless or small, but these things can spiral out of control. We are led astray by the little things and gradually, or rapidly, commit more and more sin.

Jesus explained this to the disciples, "He who *is* faithful in *what is* least is faithful also in much; and he who is unjust in *what is* least is unjust also in much" (Lk. 16:10).

Read Second Samuel eleven. Here, David sins in the beginning by remaining in Jerusalem when he should have been in battle. This progresses into adultery with Bathsheba and then murder of her husband. Uriah, Bathsheba's husband, was a loyal soldier. When David instructed him to go to his house, Uriah refused and slept at the door of the king's house. When David asked Uriah why he didn't go home, he responded, "The ark and Israel and Judah are dwelling in tents, and my lord Joab and the servants of my lord are encamped in the open fields. Shall I then go to my house to eat and drink, and to lie with my wife? *As* you live, and *as* your soul lives, I will not do this thing" (2 Samuel 11:11).

This must have made David feel a little like Saul. Here was a man defying him by doing what David should have been doing—being with his men in battle. So, David then made Uriah drink, get drunk, and lie with the servants. (See the story of Lot and his daughters in Genesis 19:33). David then sent Uriah back into battle with instructions to have him killed.

Second Samuel eleven ends, "But the thing that David had done displeased the Lord" (v. 27b).

> "And if you have not been faithful in what is another man's, who will give you what is your own" (Lk. 16:12).

Be faithful in the little things, and be careful of considering any sin to be minor, as it can lead to a multitude.

TEKOA'S WISE WOMAN

IN SECOND SAMUEL, WE SEE a nameless woman of Tekoa speak to King David, on behalf of Joab, for Absalom. Absalom had fled from Jerusalem because he had ordered David's son to be killed. David's son had raped Absalom's daughter years prior. This woman not only urged King David to have Absalom return, but she prophesied regarding God.

> "For we will surely die and *become* like water spilled on the ground, which cannot be gathered up again. Yet God does not take away a life; but He devises means, so that His banished ones are not expelled from Him" (2 Sam. 14:14).

In the New Testament, we see that this prophesy refers to God's only Son's death on the cross. This is the only way that we are not condemned for our sin. In the same way that David forgave Absalom for the murder of his son, God forgives us for our sin.

> "He has appeared to put away sin by the sacrifice of Himself. And as it is appointed for men to die once, but after this the judgment, so Christ was offered once to bear the sins of many" (Heb. 9:26b-28a).

Jesus was sacrificed for a lost world so that we wouldn't be banished from God. Through Jesus, we have the opportunity to be in a relationship with God.

THE WAR WITHIN

WHEN I WAS YOUNGER, I never even gave thought to the war that was being waged for my soul. The deception was that the war did not even exist. I simply pursued what made me feel good and was ignorant of the consequences to myself or those who loved me.

Your enemy will turn those who genuinely love you into enemies in your mind. Blind to my own selfishness, I felt and believed that those who struggled with me were the enemy. When I got saved, I realized those I saw as enemies were my only true friends.

A friend will call you out when you have done wrong. Any attempt to fight this war on your own strength is futile. The flesh is weak; the will is weak; and we fall often. Jesus shed His blood for us and won the war a long time ago. This does not stop the enemy from trying to convince us that we are losing. We are not a defeated people. When we actually believe this, Satan is left powerless to penetrate our thoughts. Jesus gave authority to the additional seventy He appointed.

> "Then the seventy returned with joy, saying, 'Lord, even the demons are subject to us in Your name.' And He said to them, 'I saw Satan fall like lightning from heaven. Behold, I give you the authority to trample on serpents and scorpions, and over all the power of the enemy, and nothing shall by any means hurt you" (Lk. 10:17-19).

WHAT IS YOUR PASSION?

A FRIEND, A MASTER CARPENTER, asked me if I was passionate about carpentry. I had been working carpentry for five years at this point, but I don't think that I was ever passionate about it. I enjoyed it, but my heart was not in it. This friend also told me to get a book called, *What Color is Your Parachute?* It is designed to help individuals find a career that matches them. The truth is that I have no desire or passion for any parachute. I believe we place too much importance on what we do to make a living. We are all flying around, looking at people's parachutes and falling in love with parachutes, instead of with the person. I want to be the man standing on the ground, pointing at Jesus. He is my Parachute. I will not spend my time trying to create my own.

> "He who observes the wind will not sow, And he who regards the clouds will not reap. As you do not know what *is* the way of the wind, *Or* how the bones grow in the *womb* of her who is with child, So you do not know the works of God who makes everything" (Eccl. 11:4-5).

God calls us to recklessly abandon the things of this world and to be passionate about Him. Let Him work out the details.

ASK AND RECEIVE

OUR INDEPENDENCE AND PRIDE KEEP us from asking and receiving from God. Also, God will only give us the things we ask for in truth. The motive behind our asking should be pure. King Solomon asked God for an understanding heart to judge the Israelites.

> "Then God said to him: 'Because you have asked this thing, and have not asked for long life for yourself, nor have asked riches for yourself, nor have asked the life of your enemies, but have asked for yourself understanding to discern justice, behold, I have done according to your words; see, I have given you a wise and discerning heart, so that there has not been anyone like you before you. And I have also given you what you have not asked: both riches and honor, so that there shall not be anyone like you among the kings all your days'" (1 Kings 3:11-13).

You see, Solomon's primary concern was justice and understanding of God's people. His motives were pure, therefore God not only grants Solomon wisdom, but also gives him riches, honor, and long life. You see, we often ask for the wrong things. Our primary concern should be promoting God's Kingdom and doing justice in a fallen world.

> "But seek first the kingdom of God and His righteousness, and all these things shall be added to you" (Matt. 6:33).

THE TEMPLE

IN THE OLD TESTAMENT, THE temple was the house where the Israelites would store the Ark of the Covenant. Solomon followed the instructions he received to build a house for the Lord. It would take seven years to build.

In the New Testament, the temple was Jesus Christ, the Son of God. Jesus was God's embodiment in human form. He died on the cross and rose again so that God could take His place in the hearts of men. It is only through Jesus that we have access to the Father. Our bodies are the temple. The Holy Spirit dwells in us.

> "But Solomon built Him a house. However, the Most High does not dwell in temples made with hands" (Acts 7:47-48a)

We tend to put a high priority on buildings that we meet in. The early church went from house to house, and they understood that the meeting place was not important. What mattered was that they all carried the Holy Spirit wherever they went. The same problem exists today. The people of God need to realize that the power of God is flowing inside of them wherever they go.

INDEPENDENCE

WE HAVE BECOME A NATION of independent individuals, who pursue their own happiness with pride. Our society tries to engrain in us the idea that freedom can be found in material things, wealth, and detachment from others. As we walk underneath the umbrella of independence, we wonder why God's blessings seem to be falling around us, yet we do not receive. This is like wondering why you aren't getting wet in a rainstorm when you are carrying a huge umbrella.

God does not bless those who are fighting for their own interests. We must be fighting for humans to become more dependent on God. Chuck your umbrella, and start walking in the rain of His presence. I pray that He will drench you and renew your strength repeatedly. The spirit of mankind was created to soar in dependence on God, not to wallow in depression underneath a spirit of independence.

> "John answered and said, 'A man can receive nothing unless it has been given to him from heaven'" (Jn. 3:27).

We should be dependent on Jesus, as Jesus is dependent on the Father.

> "Then Jesus answered and said to them, 'Most assuredly, I say to you, the Son can do nothing of Himself, but what He sees the Father do; for whatever He does, the Son also does in like manner" (Jn. 5:19).

What an image of dependence and connection! We should hunger for this kind of relationship with the Father.

LOVE

PURE LOVE WILL SACRIFICE TO the utmost—not looking for the glory, the satisfaction, or even the slightest recognition but to lift another person up with reckless disregard for oneself. When is the last time you sacrificed for others? When was the last time you cared about others? My own shortcomings are very apparent. True love is at the heart of God. Will my own heart ever get there? The desire is there, but something holds me back.

Burn away all my selfishness, God. Strip me bare, and let me experience this Love. A glimpse is not enough. I want more, and I ache for love. Fantasies are far from the reality that rips me apart. Let's start over, and this time You, God, can direct my path. Let love rise from every part of my being. Raise the roof of my spirit.

JEALOUS GOD

WHEN YOU THINK OF THE attributes of God, jealousy is not the first thing that comes to mind. However, when God made a covenant with Moses, He clearly said:

> "For you shall worship no other god, for the LORD, whose name *is* Jealous, *is* a jealous God" (Exod. 34:14).

God's desire is for us to walk with Him. Think of God as the Father of the bride. A father wants the best for his daughter. God's intention was for Israel to be in covenant with Him. The Israelites constantly went after other gods and perversions, driving God to a jealous anger.

> "For the Lord will strike Israel, as a reed is shaken in the water. He will uproot Israel from this good land which He gave to their fathers, and will scatter them beyond the River, because they have made their wooden images, provoking the Lord to anger" (1 Kings 14:15).

God sent His Son, Jesus, to give us a model of how we can walk with Him. The wedding ceremony took place at the cross. There, Christ was sacrificed for each and every one of us. Jesus' blood spilled to show the magnitude of God's love. The love between a man and a woman pales in comparison to this. Our God is a jealous God, Who desires the best for us.

> "For thus says the High and Lofty One Who inhabits eternity, Whose name *is* Holy: 'I dwell in the high and holy *place*, With *him* who has a contrite and humble spirit, To revive the spirit of the humble, And to revive the heart of the contrite ones'" (Isa. 57:15).

RAVEN'S REVIVAL

IN 1 KINGS 17, ELIJAH heard the voice of God. Elijah also spoke out against Ahab, the king of Israel at the time. After this, God tells Elijah to hide by a brook and that the ravens will feed him or bring him food.

> "The ravens brought him bread and meat in the morning, and bread and meat in the evening; and he drank from the brook" (1 Kings 17:6).

PBS did a special on ravens in which they described them as "one of the most intelligent birds having a less than savory reputation. These all black creatures acquired their dual and contradictory images—as birds of both life and death." In this chapter of the Bible, God shows us how he uses His creation to accomplish His purpose.

After the ravens along came the widow from Sidon. Sidon was an evil land, a dark place upon which God chose to shine His light. The widow's son died, and God allowed Elijah to revive him.

> "Then the woman said to Elijah, 'Now by this I know that you *are* a man of God, *and* that the word of the Lord in your mouth *is* the truth'" (1 Kings 17:24).

God tested Elijah, and Elijah did according to the Word of the Lord. When the Word of the Lord is in our mouth, people will notice our sincerity and truth. The Word of the Lord will be accompanied by signs confirming the truth of that Word.

FISHERMEN

JESUS CHOSE SEVERAL FISHERMEN TO be His disciples. He asked these men to do one thing and then made them a promise.

> "Then He said to them, 'Follow Me, and I will make you fishers of men'" (Matt. 4:19).

The same invitation and promise exists today. If you follow Jesus and share your life with unsaved people, they will take notice and want what you have. In fishing, the joy is in the catch and the fight. The true joy of being a fisher of men or women is getting to see them saved and transformed by God.

We are instructed to be fruitful and multiply. During your week, do you spend any time with unsaved people, or do you surround yourself with Christians? Sometimes, I think we are too concerned with our personal spiritual circumstances, and we don't reach out to our lost friends, family, co-workers, acquaintances, enemies, etc. Jesus calls us to be the light of the world; don't hide that light! To follow Christ is to become a fisherman.

> "Again, the kingdom of heaven is like a dragnet that was cast into the sea and gathered some of every kind, which, when it was full, they drew to the shore; and they sat down and gathered the good into vessels, but threw the bad away" (Matt. 13:47-48).

Our goal should be to reach lost souls for the kingdom of heaven. As a consequence of reaching out to others, our spirits will be lifted.

CHARIOTS OF FIRE

I REMEMBER WATCHING A MOVIE called *Chariots of Fire* when I was a child. The movie was a story about Olympic runners, but it was also about faith. A runner experiences both pain and joy during a race. Our faith will encounter the same.

> "Let us lay aside every weight, and the sin which so easily ensnares *us,* and let us run with endurance the race that is set before us, looking unto Jesus, the author and finisher of *our* faith, who for the joy that was set before Him endured the cross, despising the shame, and has sat down at the right hand of the throne of God" (Heb. 12:1-2).

We are told that Elijah was a man of great faith and that he pleased God. He was a runner who endured to the end. Elijah's departure from earth was a miraculous one.

> "Then it happened, as they continued on and talked, that suddenly a chariot of fire *appeared* with horses of fire, and separated the two of them: and Elijah went up by a whirlwind into heaven" (2 Kings 2:11).

Are you running the race with endurance and strength?

WIELDING THE SWORD

JEHU, THE COMMANDER OF THE Israeli army during the reign of the house of Ahab, was anointed to be the new king of Israel and to take vengeance for God against both Joram, king of Israel, and Ahaziah, king of Judah. As Jehu approached Jezreel, where both kings were staying, Joram sent out two horsemen to see if Jehu came in peace.

> "So the horsemen went to meet him and said, 'Thus says the king: *Is it peace?*" And Jehu said, 'What have you to do with peace? Turn around and follow me.' So the watchman reported, saying, 'The messenger went to them, but is not coming back'" (2 Kings 9:18).

After another horseman went out and didn't return, the king suited up and went out. Jehu killed both kings and Jezebel as the Lord instructed through His prophet Elisha.

Oftentimes, we will go out to God, looking for peace and ending up abandoning everything to follow Him. When Jesus instructed the twelve disciples, He stated, "Do not think that I came to bring peace on earth. I did not come to bring peace but a sword" (Matt. 10:34).

Our sword today is the Word of God.

> "For the word of God *is* living and powerful, and sharper than any two-edged sword, piercing even to the division of soul and spirit, and of joints and marrow, and is a discerner of the thoughts and intents of the heart" (Heb. 4:12).

Many people search for peace today but are unwilling to be pierced by God's Word. To be in God's will, we must first take up His Word and use it on ourselves.

METANOEO

CHANGE YOUR MIND

HOW OFTEN DO I TRULY repent for sin? True repentance will reflect a change in your life. The Greek word for repentance is Metanoeo, and it signifies changing one's mind or purpose. When we confess our sins to God, it often hurts, and we can even shed tears over our sin. But if we don't actually change our way of thinking, we will find ourselves back in the place of confession and heartache again.

> "As a dog returns to his own vomit, *So* a fool repeats
> his folly" (Prov. 26:11).

God has given everyone a brain to use and free will to choose. Are you choosing to be changed or settling for the simple pleasures of a life lived in selfish pursuits? I desire change in my own life. I desire change in the world I live in. Desires alone will not create a change in myself or the world around me. God says to us believers:

> "As many as I love, I rebuke and chasten. Therefore
> be zealous and repent" (Rev. 3:19).

We can get used to repeated confession and become numb to our sin, or we can take the road less traveled and truly repent and become transformed people.

TWO BY TWO

IN CHAPTER TEN OF LUKE, we see Jesus appointing an additional seventy others to go out into every city. He gave them power to heal the sick and cast out demons.

> "Then He said to them, 'The harvest truly *is* great, but the laborers *are* few; therefore pray the Lord of the harvest to send out laborers into His harvest. Go your way; behold, I send you out as lambs among wolves. Carry neither money bag, knapsack, nor sandals; and greet no one along the road'" (Lk. 10:2-4).

Our faith is an endurance race. We will endure much farther when we are encouraged by one other brother or sister. Alone, we tend to give up much sooner than when we have someone pushing us or challenging us. This is the reason Jesus sent them out in twos. We are His laborers, and we must be ready to go out into the field. He will give us power, but He also warns us:

> "Nevertheless do not rejoice in this, that the spirits are subject to you, but rather rejoice because your names are written in heaven" (Lk. 10:20).

Jesus is calling us to have compassion for the lost and hurting around us. Don't put His call on hold!

> "But Jesus said to him, 'No one, having put his hand to the plow, and looking back, is fit for the kingdom of God'" (Lk. 9:62).

HOLDING YOUR PEACE

SENNACHERIB, KING OF ASSYRIA, THREATENED the kingdom of Judah during the reign of Hezekiah. Sennacherib sent messengers to discourage God's people and king Hezekiah from opposing Him. Sennacherib's repeated attempts to demoralize Hezekiah and the people failed because they held their peace.

> "But the people held their peace and answered him not a word; for the king's commandment was, 'Do not answer him'" (2 Kings 18:36).

Sometimes, God calls us to remain quiet when we are tempted. When we open our mouths, we give Satan grounds to work against us. Submit every thought to God before speaking it. You may find that you speak much less; but your peace will increase, and your sight and hearing will enhance.

ELEVATE

WORDS DO NOT BRING JUSTICE or sufficient explanation of a single experience with our God. These moments are when He elevates our spirit, and we are suspended in the shadow of His presence. Time ceases to exist, and we are experiencing the truth of being alive in the rawest form. The past and future cease to matter for these moments. I long to live in this elevated place forever. All other moments pale in comparison. Joy is inexpressible and uncontainable. When we worship Him, He gives us these moments. They are refreshing experiences. Peter explained to the people:

> "Repent therefore and be converted, that your sins may be blotted out, so that times of refreshing may come from the presence of the Lord, and that He may send Jesus Christ, who was preached to you before, whom heaven must receive until the times of restoration of all things, which God has spoken by the mouth of all His holy prophets since the world began" (Acts 3:19-21).

God will restore and elevate all things. One day, these elevated moments will become eternal worship and perpetual joy.

> "Now it came to pass, while He blessed them, that He was parted from them and carried up into heaven. And they worshipped Him, and returned to Jerusalem with great joy, and were continually in the temple praising and blessing God. Amen" (Lk. 24:51-53).

LOVING YOUR NEIGHBOR

HOW MANY OF YOUR NEIGHBORS' names do you know? These are the people you will cross paths with every day. These are the people God has placed around you. How can we begin to love our neighbors if we haven't even taken the time to introduce ourselves? God commands His children to love Him with all their "heart, soul, and strength" (Deuteronomy 6:5). This is our first step in following after God. God gave Moses instructions for the people on how to follow Him.

> "You shall not take vengeance, nor bear any grudge against the children of your people, but you shall love your neighbor as yourself; I *am* the Lord" (Lev. 19:18).

The way we properly love ourselves is by loving God, and the way to love God is to love others. It is only possible to love your neighbors when you truly come to love God. And then, through Jesus, we can go even deeper. During Jesus's Sermon on the Mount, He said to His disciples:

> "You have heard that it was said, 'You shall love your neighbor and hate your enemy.' But I say to you, love your enemies, bless those who curse you, do good to those who hate you, and pray for those who spitefully use you and persecute you" (Matt. 5:43-44).

It's easy to love an Almighty God; it's possible to love your neighbor; and it's only through the resurrected life of Jesus in us that we can love our enemies.

CHILD'S PLAY

I HAD MY FIRST PLAYFUL experience with God today. As I saw the sun rising over the ocean, I felt my body tremble and stop. And then start again. As I opened His Word, it hit me again. In my mind, I was telling God, "I'm trying to be serious." I heard Him respond, "Oh, okay," and then playfully do it again. It reminded me of when we used to laugh so hard, we would cry and hold our stomachs in pain. The laughter would subside for a brief time and then explode again. This was a strong reminder to me that I am a child of God. When the disciples asked Jesus who is the greatest in the kingdom of God, He sat a little child in their midst and said:

> "Assuredly, I say to you, unless you are converted and become as little children, you will by no means enter the kingdom of heaven" (Matt. 18:3).

THE CHOSEN FAST

GOD IS CALLING US—NOT TO afflict our own souls, but to raise up the afflicted souls of others.

> "*Is* this not the fast that I have chosen: To loose the bonds of wickedness, To undo the heavy burdens, To let the oppressed go free, And that you break every yoke? *Is it* not to share your bread with the hungry, and that you bring to your house the poor who are cast out; When you see the naked, that you cover him, And not hide yourself from your own flesh? Then your light shall break forth like the morning, Your healing shall spring forth speedily, And your righteousness shall go before you; The glory of the Lord shall be your rear guard" (Isa. 58:6-8).

It is important that our heart is pure in whatever we do. God sees our motives; and if they are not right, our actions are ineffective. Isaiah clearly declares God's will for us. We are to work against wickedness, bondage, poverty, and oppression—not just in our own lives, but in those who are lost and hurting around us. When we do this, the glory of the Lord will be about us, and His light will shine through us.

DISCONNECT AND RECONNECT

IT IS POSSIBLE TO BE connected, yet feel disconnected. The phone, the internet, text messaging, and emailing have made this possible. How is it that we can be plugged into all these forms of communication and still feel lonely at the end of the day? The reason is because all this technology has not brought us closer together but rather has allowed us to cope with being alone. It is like putting a Band-Aid on a gushing wound. It may stop the bleeding for a while, but it won't heal the wound.

Scripture provides a better explanation, going back to the beginning of creation. "And the Lord God said, '*It is* not good that man should be alone; I will make him a helper comparable to him" (Gen. 2:18). God the Father recognized Adam's need for companionship. It is a need that is present in everyone's life, without exception. It is important to spend time disconnecting from all the technology that fights for our attention and reconnecting with God. At the Last Supper, Jesus informed His disciples about how they would leave Him alone.

> "Indeed the hour is coming, yes, has now come, that you will be scattered, each to his own, and will leave Me alone. And yet I am not alone, because the Father is with Me" (Jn. 16:32).

First and foremost, God is the only One Who can heal our loneliness. We were created to fellowship with Him. When we connect with Him, we will not feel alone. A companion is an additional gift from God. We must first learn to be complete in Him before we are ready for this gift.

WARFARE

THE OLD TESTAMENT IS FULL of wars and battles fought by men. We see God's hand moving in victory for those who follow Him and destruction on those who oppose Him. We see David's army grow in numbers and might only when he is submitted to God. When David is a fugitive in Ziklag, men of every tribe come to Him and submit to Him because they know God is on David's side.

> "And David went out to meet them, and answered and said to them, 'If you have come peaceably to me to help me, my heart will be united with you; but if to betray me to my enemies, since *there is* no wrong in my hands, may the God of our fathers look and bring judgment" (1 Chron. 12:17).

In the New Testament and today, the army of God is the Church. And our warfare is defined by Paul.

> "For we do not wrestle against flesh and blood, but against principalities, against powers, against the rulers of the darkness of this age, against spiritual *hosts* of wickedness in the heavenly *places*" (Eph. 6:12).

Jesus crucified the flesh on the cross, and through faith in Him, we find our salvation. Our battle is no longer against man but against the powers of darkness that oppress the spirit of man.

FEAR AND HUMILITY

WE ARE COMMANDED TO WALK in fear and humility before God. When David brought the ark of God from Judah, he was afraid of God.

> "David was afraid of God that day, saying, 'How can I bring the ark of God to me'" (1 Chron. 13:12).

David's fear was appropriate, but notice that it says "that day." How often do you stay in that place of fear? David went on to build a great house, took many wives, and conquered the Philistines. God allowed all of this.

> "Then the fame of David went out into all lands, and the Lord brought the fear of him upon all nations" (1 Chron. 14:17).

When we fear God and humble ourselves before Him, He will lift us up.

> "Humble yourselves in the sight of the Lord, and He will lift you up" (Jas. 4:10).

The hardest part is to remain humble as God lifts you up. The key to remaining humble is to remind yourself constantly that everything you are, have, or will ever become is because of God.

> "God, who made the world and everything in it, since He is Lord of heaven and earth, does not dwell in temples made with hands. Nor is He worshiped with men's hands, as though He needed anything, since He gives to all life, breath, and all things" (Acts 17:24-25).

Let us remain humble as He moves in us.

PURPOSE OF WORSHIP

THE PURPOSE OF WORSHIP IS to bring God glory. It is a special way we can show our gratitude for what God has done and continues to do for us. Like the Levites of old, some people are skilled in worship.

> "Chenaniah, leader of the Levites, was instructor *in charge of* the music, because he *was* skillful" (1 Chron. 15:22).

We can be skilled in certain areas, but it is important to always be aware that all our skills are given by God. This should keep us in a state of constant thankfulness. When the ark of God was brought into the tabernacle of David, he used the skills of his people

> "And he appointed some of the Levites to minister before the ark of the LORD, to commemorate, to thank, and to praise the LORD God of Israel" (1 Chron. 16:4).

Each time we come before God, we should be ministering in this way through worship.

> "Enter into His gates with thanksgiving, *And* into His courts with praise. Be thankful to Him, *and* bless His name" (Psa. 100:4).

WHO AM I?

THE STORY OF DAVID'S LIFE prompts him to constantly ask God this question. I often find myself asking this question when I look at who I used to be—He brought me to Himself. David was a lowly shepherd, but God took him away from that life.

> "I took you from the sheepfold, from following the sheep, to be ruler over My people Israel" (1 Chron. 17:7b).

Nathan was not only David's friend, but he was also the prophet of his time. Nathan informed David that God was going to bring forth His kingdom from David's seed. The very Son of God would come from David's lineage. David was obviously blown away by this.

> "Then King David went in and sat before the Lord; and he said: 'Who *am* I, O LORD God? And what is my house, that You have brought me this far" (1 Chron. 17:16).

Sometimes, what God pours out on us is so powerful and beyond what we ever imagined would happen to us that our only response is to come sit before Him and ask, "Who am I?"

HIS MOONLIGHT

THE SUN BURNS BRIGHT DURING these hours of daylight, allowing us to see the world around us and the mission field He has called us to. When darkness descends, a different kind of light shines forth from that initial sliver of a moon. This intense white light glows around the dark surroundings and is reflected on drifting clouds and the surface of the ocean. The sun is always the same size, but the moon has a cycle. A full moon shines forth God's glory. While there is still daylight and moonlight, we are called to spread His Word to all the nations.

> "And this gospel of the kingdom will be preached in all the world as a witness to all the nations, and then the end will come" (Matt. 24:14).

We are told great tribulations will follow this.

> "Immediately after the tribulation of those days the sun will be darkened, and the moon will not give its light; the stars will fall from heaven, and the powers of the heavens will be shaken" (Matt. 24:29).

> "Then, I John, saw the holy city, New Jerusalem, coming down out of heaven from God, prepared as a bride adorned for her husband" (Rev. 21:2).

> "The city had no need of the sun or of the moon to shine in it, for the glory of God illuminated it. The Lamb *is* its light" (Rev. 21:23).

LOYAL HEART

HOW LOYAL AM I TO God? Am I loyal only when it feels good, or am I loyal when it feels like I'm being dragged through the mud? The true test of loyalty comes when times are tough. True friends are there for you in the down times. God calls us to be loyal to His heart. We are to love the things that He loves. David instructed his son, Solomon, in this way.

> "As for you, my son Solomon, know the God of your father, and serve Him with a loyal heart and with a willing mind; for the LORD searches all hearts and understands all the intent of the thoughts. If you seek Him, He will be found by you; but if you forsake Him, He will cast you off forever" (1 Chron. 28:9).

David was a man after God's own heart, and he suffered loyally. Jesus was God in human form, and He was loyal to the death. A loyal heart has no limits. At Gethsemane, Jesus expressed His sorrow and His loyalty.

> "Then He said to them, 'My soul is exceedingly sorrowful, even to death. Stay here and watch with Me.'; He went a little farther and fell on His face, and prayed, saying, 'O My Father, if it is possible, let this cup pass from Me; nevertheless, not as I will, but as You *will*" (Matt. 26:38-39).

Loyalty is never easy, but nothing great ever came from anything easy. Submit to Him, and be loyal to Him, and He will establish greatness in your heart.

THE POTTER AND THE CLAY

WE ARE THE DUST GOD forms into clumps of clay to build vessels that His Spirit can dwell in. The vessel is a thing of beauty, but it doesn't get there without severe pounding and molding. Sometimes, the Potter has to destroy the vessel and start over. It is in these times that our deepest pain is felt, and we need to hold on to the faith that God knows what's best for us.

> "Your hands have made me and fashioned me, An intricate unity; Yet You would destroy me. Remember, I pray, that You have made me like clay. And will You turn me into dust again? Did you not pour me out like milk, And curdle me like cheese, Clothe me with skin and flesh, and knit me together with bones and sinews? You have granted me life and favor, and Your care has preserved my spirit" (Job 10:8-12).

One of the ways we can assist our Potter is by walking in the light. When we decide to walk into the darkness, He will wait for our return to His marvelous light. In the darkness, we are tricked into believing that we can mold ourselves.

> Woe to those who seek deep to hide their counsel far from the LORD, and their works are in the dark; They say, "Who sees us?" and, "Who knows us?" Surely you have things turned around! Shall the potter be esteemed as the clay; For shall the thing made say of him who made it, "He did not make me"? or shall the thing formed say of him who formed it, "He has no understanding"? (Isa. 29:15-16).

Keep us in Your light and do what You will, My Lord, My King!

GOD'S CLOUD

THERE ARE 108 VERSES IN the Bible containing the word "cloud." In both the Old and New Testaments, we see God interact with man through a cloud. The cloud is a filter for the glory of the Lord. Moses interacted with God on several occasions through this cloud.

In Exodus, Moses pleaded with God, "Please, show me Your glory" (Exod. 33:18). "But [God] said, 'You cannot see My face; for no man shall see Me, and live" (Exod. 33:20). God delivered the commandments to Moses; they were placed in the ark; and they came to dwell in the temple built by Solomon. The Levites and priests began to sing and worship with stringed instruments and then "the house of the Lord was filled with a cloud, so that the priests could not continue ministering because of the cloud; for the glory of the Lord filled the house of God" (2 Chron. 5:13b-14).

We get the sense of God's glory, masked by His cloud. Small doses of His glory are all we can handle for now.

> "For now we see in a mirror, dimly, but then face to face. Now I know in part, but then I shall know just as I also am known" (1 Cor. 13:12).

Please show us your Glory, God!

ELDERLY ADVICE AND HEAVY YOKES

WE ARE QUICK TO RUN to our peers for advice. We often seek counsel from those who will tell us what we want to hear and not what we need to hear. Rehoboam, Solomon's son, made the same mistake. At first, he sought the advice of the elders, but when he didn't hear what he wanted to hear, he went to his peers.

> "But he rejected the advice which the elders had given him, and consulted the young men who had grown up with him, who stood before him" (2 Chron. 10:8).

Rehoboam took the advice of the young men to treat the people of Israel harshly. The people of Israel had said, "Your father made our yoke heavy; now therefore, lighten the burdensome service of your father and his heavy yoke which he put on us, and we will serve you" (2 Chron. 10:4).

Rehoboam rejected them, "So Israel has been in rebellion against the house of David to this day" (2 Chron. 10:19).

The son of the *human* king Solomon was not merciful, but the Son of our *eternal* King is full of mercy and love.

> "Come to Me, all *you* who labor and are heavy laden, and I will give you rest. Take My yoke upon you and learn from Me; for I am gentle and lowly in heart, and you will find rest for your souls. For My yoke *is* easy and My burden is light" (Matt. 11:28-30).

PIERCING ARROWS

THE OLD TESTAMENT IS FULL of prophets who shared the truth and suffered for it. Micaiah, a prophet of Israel, was hated by King Ahab. Ahab wanted to partner with Jehoshaphat, king of Judah, to go up against Ramoth Gilead. Jehoshaphat wanted to hear from God, so Ahab gathered 400 prophets who would say that God would give them favor. Jehoshaphat requested a prophet of the Lord from Ahab.

> "So the king of Israel said to Jehoshaphat, '*There is* still one man by whom we may inquire of the LORD; but I hate him, because he never prophesies good concerning me, but always evil. He *is* Micaiah the son of Imla" (2 Chron. 18:7).

Micaiah spoke the truth, saying that Ahab would fall at Ramoth Gilead. For this, Micaiah was struck and imprisoned. Ahab went up to Ramoth Gilead and disguised himself to avoid what the Lord had spoken out against him. But his disguise didn't work.

> "Now a certain man drew a bow at random, and struck the king of Israel between the joints of his armor" (2 Chron. 18:33a).

At sunset, Ahab died. Oftentimes, we think we can avoid God's wrath and justice by hiding. Ahab thought he was clever, but what we see is ignorance. Be careful of not heeding God's warnings and believing that you can hide from Him. Our God is loving, but He also sees and knows all things. His arrows never miss their target.

> "For the wrath of God is revealed from heaven against all ungodliness and unrighteousness of men, who suppress the truth in unrighteousness" (Rom. 1:18).

SHIFTING WINDS

THE WIND IS AN EXAMPLE to us of how God moves. We cannot see the wind, but we can feel it and observe how it affects the things it touches. In the clearing of a Hawaiian field, I sat and watched the wind blow patches of tall weeds in different directions. The breeze was gentle refreshment from the stagnant heat of the day. Suddenly, there was stillness. A moment passed, and a new wind blew from the opposite direction. The weeds swayed into this new direction.

> "Behold, the whirlwind of the Lord Goes forth with fury, A continuing whirlwind; It will fall violently on the head of the wicked. The fierce anger of the Lord will not return until He has done it, And until He has performed the intents of His heart. In the latter days you will consider it" (Jer. 30:23-24).

There were approximately 400 years between the Old and New Testament—a time of shifting winds and silence. The intents of God's heart would be manifested through His only Son, Jesus. John the Baptist was God's messenger, speaking of the coming of the Messiah.

" . . . Jesus began to say to the multitudes concerning John: 'What did you go out in the wilderness to see? A reed shaken by the wind?'" (Matt. 11:7). John only spoke the words that God's Spirit placed there.

Forty days after His resurrection, Jesus ascended to be with the Father. For a period of ten days, the disciples experienced a stillness and quiet, until the day of Pentecost.

"And suddenly there came a sound from heaven, as
of a rushing mighty wind, and it filled the whole
house where they were sitting" (Acts 2:2).

John was a man who felt God's Spirit in the wilderness.
Because of what Jesus did for us on the cross, we can experience God's Spirit in any setting. If you are in a season of stillness or silence, be aware that this is only a period where God
may be shifting the winds of His Spirit within you.

"The wind blows where it wishes, and you hear the
sound of it, but cannot tell where it comes from
and where it goes. So is everyone who is born of
the Spirit" (Jn. 3:8).

THE TEMPLE

JOASH CAME TO BE KING at the age of seven. "Joash did *what was* right in the sight of the Lord all the days of Jehoiada the priest" (2 Chron. 24:2).

Joash set his heart to repair the temple. He gathered money from the people and hired masons and carpenters to restore the house of the Lord.

> "So the workmen labored, and the work was completed by them: they restored the house of God to its original condition and reinforced it" (2 Chron. 24:13).

When Jehoiada, the priest, died, the leaders came to Joash, bowed down to him, and led him away from God.

> "Therefore they left the house of the LORD God of their fathers, and served wooden images and idols; and wrath came upon Judah and Jerusalem because of their trespass" (2 Chron. 24:18).

The building was repaired, but the people's hearts were turned away. God's pleasure is not found in structures built by men but rather in the hearts of men and women. Jesus cautioned against only changing the outward appearance in Matthew.

> Woe to you, scribes and Pharisees, hypocrites! For you cleanse the outside of the cup and dish, but inside they are full of extortion and self-indulgence. Blind Pharisee, first cleanse the inside of the cup and dish, that the outside of them may be clean also. Woe to you, scribes and Pharisees, hypocrites! For you are like whitewashed tombs which indeed

appear beautiful outwardly, but inside are full of
dead *men's* bones and all uncleanness (Matt. 23:25-27).

If we are more concerned about our appearance to others
than our appearance to God, His Spirit cannot work in and
through us. Forget what others may see or think and start
being more concerned with the condition of your heart. God
doesn't receive from the work of our hands. The temple was
destroyed on the cross, and in that moment, God purchased
the right to our hearts.

PROSPERITY OR PROSPER?

WHEN THE LEADERS OF ISRAEL walked away from God to pursue wooden images and idols, they experienced God's wrath. At the same time, God sent a prophet to speak to them.

> "Then the Spirit of God came upon Zechariah the son of Jehoiada the priest, who stood above the people, and said to them, 'Thus says God: *Why do you transgress the commandments of the LORD, so that you cannot prosper? Because you have forsaken the LORD, He also has forsaken you*'" (2 Chron. 24:20).

The leaders agreed to stone and kill this prophet. Speaking God's Word and experiencing His Spirit upon you is powerful, but not always pleasant. Zechariah was killed after God's Spirit came upon him. He was obedient to what he had been called and the kingdom of God would prosper.

Jeremiah wrote a letter to the elders, who became captives in Babylon. In the letter, he delivers God's message to them.

> For thus says the Lord: After seventy years are completed at Babylon, I will visit you and perform My good word toward you, and cause you to return to this place. For I know the thoughts that I think toward you, says the LORD, thoughts of peace and not of evil, to give you a future and a hope. Then you will call upon Me, and go and pray to Me, and I will listen to you. And you will seek Me and find *Me*, when you search for Me with all your heart (Jer. 29:10-13).

God's plan for us hasn't changed. We are His exiled people, living in a modern-day Babylon. He wants to give us peace, hope, and a future. He wants to prosper His kingdom. He wants us to cry out to Him in prayer and to seek Him. How consumed are you with your own personal prosperity? When you seek Him and find Him, prosperity becomes dull compared to a life lived in service to God.

Psalm 34

Quick to speak.

Quick to write.

Slow to Fight.

The Lord gives power and might, not hopelessness and flight

He delivers me from all evil.

He hears my cry in the night.

Tears away the distractions and makes me whole.

Equips me for battle and guards my soul.

A tool in the hands of my Maker, I become effective as He uses me.

"Many *are* the afflictions of the righteous, But the LORD delivers him out of them all" (Psa. 34:19).

DESTRUCTIVE STRENGTH

WHEN WE TAKE OUR EYES off of God and start to believe that we have our own strength, we are bound to be humbled. We need to remember that every good and perfect gift comes from above, from our Father of lights. King Uzziah lost sight of this.

> "So his fame spread far and wide, for he was marvelously helped till he became strong. But when he was strong his heart was lifted up, to *his* destruction, for he transgressed against the LORD his God by entering the temple of the Lord to burn incense on the altar of incense" (2 Chron. 26:15b-16).

Eighty priests confront him and rebuke him for his trespass.

> "Then Uzziah became furious; and he *had* a censer in his hand to burn incense. And while he was angry with the priests, leprosy broke out on his forehead, before the priests in the house of the LORD, beside the incense altar" (2 Chron. 26:19).

Only one is strong, and our strength comes from Him. We must respect, fear, and honor Him. Our strength becomes destructive when it is no longer a reflection of God but of our own self-seeking pride. The consequences are often humility, sorrow, and pain, or even death.

Samson was a man of great strength.

> "And the Spirit of the Lord came mightily upon him, and he tore the lion apart as one would have torn

apart a young goat, though *he had* nothing in his
hand" (Judg. 14:6a).

God had blessed Samson with a supernatural strength.
Samson believed that his strength came from his hair, but the
true source was God. When the Philistines captured him and
cut out his eyes, he prayed to the Lord for strength.

> "Then Samson said, 'Let me die with the Philistines!'
> And he pushed with *all his* might, and the temple fell
> on the lords and all the people who *were* in it. So the
> dead that he killed at his death were more than he
> had killed in his life" (Judg. 16:30).

Jesus saved more people by His death on the cross than He
would in his short lifetime on this earth. Having destroyed the
temple of His body, Jesus brought salvation to mankind from
that point forward to eternity. The Lion of Judah was torn by
the hands of men, but out of this, we have the sweetness of
our salvation. He is the only one who can open the Word to us.

> "But one of the elders said to me, 'Do not weep.
> Behold, the Lion of the tribe of Judah, the Root of
> David, has prevailed to open the scroll and to loose
> its seven seals" (Rev. 5:5).

BEARING FRUIT

DO WE LONG TO BEAR fruit? Are we hungry to see God's Word implanted in us and strengthening us? We cannot bear fruit by developing a plan or strategy of human understanding. The only way to bear fruit is to seek after God. When we become entrenched in Him, He will develop fruit in us that we don't even see. The fruits of the Spirit become alive in us when we seek God wholeheartedly.

Hezekiah did what was right in the sight of the Lord.

> "And in every work that he began in the service of the house of God, in the law and in the commandment, to seek his God, he did *it* all with all his heart. So he prospered" (2 Chron. 31:21).

When we spend time in the Word, we become nourished and begin to grow. Psalm one describes the person who meditates on the Word.

> "He shall be like a tree Planted by the rivers of water, That brings forth its fruit in its season, Whose leaf also shall not wither; And whatever he does shall prosper" (Psa. 1:3).

What are the fruit we are going to bring forth? Paul tells us in Galatians 5:22-23, "But the fruit of the Spirit is love, joy, peace, longsuffering, kindness, goodness, faithfulness, gentleness, self-control. Against such there is no law."

CRYING OUT

SOMETIMES CRYING OUT TO GOD is not the first thing that comes to mind when we face a trial. We prefer to keep silent and struggle through it. Our pride will keep us from doing the necessary thing, which is crying out. A baby has no problem crying out to his parents when he or she has a need. As adults, we are taught to be mature and bear the weights the world places on us. Don't expect to see God move powerfully if you are not crying out to Him.

When King Sennacherib came up against Israel and spoke out against God, God did not strike him down immediately.

> Now because of this King Hezekiah and the prophet Isaiah, the son of Amoz, prayed and cried out to heaven. Then the LORD sent an angel who cut down every mighty man of valor, leader, and captain in the camp of the king of Assyria. So [Sennacherib] returned shamefaced to his own land. And when he had gone into the temple of his god, some of his own offspring struck him down with the sword there (2 Chron. 32:20-21).

The king and the prophet cried out, and God sent an angel. This does not mean that every time we cry out, God will automatically send an angel. God will withdraw in certain situations to test us or allow us to exercise our faith. When ambassadors from Babylon came to inquire of Hezekiah about what God had done, " . . . God withdrew from him, in order to test him, that He might know all *that was* in his heart" (2 Chron. 32:31).

God withdrew from His only Son on the cross.

"And about the ninth hour Jesus cried out with a loud voice, saying . . . 'My God, My God, why have You forsaken Me?'" (Matt. 27:46).

Jesus cried out one last time and yielded up His spirit. The will of God was completed. He sacrificed His Son for us. God allowed His Son to cry out so that we could get a glimpse of the severity of the sacrifice. Are we still too proud to get down on our knees and cry out to Him?

TEMPTED VS. TESTED

TEMPTING AND TESTING ARE TWO different things that we
have trouble discerning sometimes. Temptation always comes
from Satan. It is always the promise of something better than
what God has for us, as though it will make you happy. Satan
tries to get us to act on these thoughts. Many of us know that
when we act on these temptations, we don't end up happy. This
is the ultimate deception.

> "Let no one say when he is tempted, "I am tempted by
> God"; for God cannot be tempted by evil, nor does He
> Himself tempt anyone. But each one is tempted when
> he is drawn away by his own desires and enticed. Then,
> when desire has conceived, it gives birth to sin; and sin
> when it is full-grown, brings forth death" (Jas. 1:13-15).

Testing comes in a different form. It does not involve any
false promises or anything alluring. Most often, it comes in
the form of a question, and then silence. The purpose is to see
not how we will answer the question, but how we will live
our answer out. Peter is a prime example of this when Jesus
asked him a pointed question.

> "So when they had eaten breakfast, Jesus said to Simon
> Peter, 'Simon, *son* of Jonah, do you love Me more than
> these?' He said to Him, 'Yes, Lord; You know that I love
> You.' He said to him, 'Feed my lambs'" (Jn. 21:15).

Testing can be hard because we feel God is at a distance, but
Scripture promises us that He will never leave us nor forsake us.

LAYING THE FOUNDATION

CYRUS, KING OF PERSIA, DECLARED that the captives of Babylon be released to complete a command of God. The command was to rebuild the temple in Jerusalem. The Israelite captives were to be set free and also given all the necessary supplies to build this temple. Upon the completion of the foundation, "Then all the people shouted with a great shout, when they praised the LORD, because the foundation of the house of the LORD was laid" (Ezra 3:11b).

Immediately after the foundation was laid, adversaries came to deceive God's people, saying, "Let us build with you, for we seek your God as you *do*" (Ezra 4:2a).

When the heads of the houses of Israel refused these adversaries, they encountered opposition, and the adversaries began to do everything in their power to stop the building of the temple. They succeeded in stopping Israel for a period.

> "Thus the work of the house of God which *is* at Jerusalem ceased, and it was discontinued until the second year of the reign of Darius king of Persia" (Ezra 4:24).

When God establishes a foundation for anything, we can expect to encounter intense opposition. We must remain faithful during the period of what can appear to be defeat. The foundation is laid; and as long as the foundation is strong, man will not be able to oppose it. Our foundation today is Jesus; and as long as we stand on Him, His Church will come forth.

> "And they kept the Feast of Unleavened Bread seven days with joy; for the LORD made them joyful, and

turned the heart of the king of Assyria toward them, to strengthen their hands in the work of the house of God, the God of Israel" (Ezra 6:22).

God can change men in powerful places.

"The king's heart *is* in the hand of the LORD, *Like* the rivers of water; He turns it wherever He wishes" (Prov. 21:1).

DO IT

THERE ARE A FEW STEPS in seeking our God. First, we have to humble ourselves and recognize that we are lost sinners who need His help. Then, we must allow Him to prepare our hearts. This means changing the way we feel, think, and interpret our lives. Some people say that the eyes are the window to the soul, but God wants the reverse for us. Our soul and heart should reflect Christ, and He should be the window through which we see this world. When we are being transformed in this way, our eyes will reflect a light like no other.

This is not the end of experiencing God. We must continue to do that which He has shown us. We can prepare our hearts and not take action. We are satisfied with experiencing personal transformation. This is purely selfish. We cannot stop at this stage. We have an obligation to share salvation. Jesus instructed His disciples to tell others about Him.

> "You are the light of the world. A city that is set on a hill cannot be hidden. Nor do they light a lamp and put it under a basket, but on a lampstand, and it gives light to all *who are* in the house. Let your light so shine before men, that they may see your good works and glorify your Father in heaven" (Matt. 5:14-16).

LEADERSHIP FASTING

FASTING TODAY IS CONSIDERED A very private and personal thing between the person fasting and God. It represents the individual's strong hunger for God and a desire to know His will. In the Old Testament, we find strong leaders declaring fasts or periods of fasting for the heads of families. Ezra said, "Then I proclaimed a fast there at the river of Ahava, that we might humble ourselves before our God, to seek from Him the right way for us and our little ones and all our possessions" (Ezra 8:21).

The Lord answers Ezra and His people and protects them from their enemies as they travel through foreign land. As the heads of the families fasted and prayed together, they received God's hand of protection.

Jesus showed us His power when He cast a demon out of a young boy. Jesus asked the father of the demon-possessed boy how long this had gone on. The father said it had been going on since childhood. The father begged Jesus for help. "Jesus said to him, 'If you can believe, all things *are* possible to him who believes'" (Mk. 9:23).

Jesus then cast out the demon. His disciples asked Jesus privately why they weren't able to cast out the demon. "So He said to them, 'This kind can come out by nothing but prayer and fasting'" (Mk. 9:29).

If we want to be disciples or leaders for God, we have to believe wholeheartedly, and we must submit to prayer and fasting for the protection and healing of this hurt and oppressed people. This is Jesus' example to us.

GOD'S HAND

THE NEW YEAR OFTEN STARTS with us making plans to improve ourselves or our financial situations. We believe that if we improve these areas, we will feel more satisfied. The truth is our focus on these areas can often lead to more dissatisfaction. It should not be our plans for improvement that take up our thoughts, but, rather, God's plans should be our top priority. When Nehemiah went before King Artaxerxes to plead for the city of Jerusalem, he prayed fiercely.

"Then the king said to me, "What do you request?" So
I prayed to the God of heaven" (Neh. 2:4).

This should be our first reaction. Pray before pursuing your own desires. Make sure it is what God wants as well. God's hand will be upon you as you are following His will. Nehemiah requested to return to Judah to rebuild the city and to be given the materials to rebuild. It seems bold for a cupbearer to ask for these things, but his request was approved.

"And the king granted *them* to me according to the
good hand of my God upon me" (Neh. 2:8b).

My desire is that God's hand would be upon me more and more. I want to experience His hand guiding and directing me the way Nehemiah experienced it.

SELFLESS LEADERSHIP

NEHEMIAH WAS APPOINTED GOVERNOR OF the people as they rebuilt the wall around Jerusalem. Nehemiah did not take advantage of any of the rights of a governor. He did not seek after food or money from the hand of the people.

> "But the former governors who *were* before me laid burdens on the people, and took from them bread and wine, besides forty shekels of silver. Yes, even their servants bore rule over the people, but I did not do so, because of the fear of God" (Neh. 5:15).

Nehemiah saw the oppression of God's people, and He decided to work alongside them and demand things from them. Leading was a burden, not a benefit. Nehemiah did not take the comfortable, easy approach; he took the selfless and sacrificial one.

"The fear of the LORD is the beginning of wisdom" (Psa. 111:10). Nehemiah did not do these things because he sought recognition but because he had a fear of God.

When Jesus walked the earth, He did not seek to impress people or rule over them. His desire was to love people and to sacrifice Himself for sinners. The religious people of that time had burdened the people with rules and monetary demands that never came from God. Jesus accused the scribes and Pharisees saying, "And in vain they worship Me, Teaching *as* doctrines the commandments of men" (Matt. 15:9).

Be careful of rules that you place on others that do not come from God. Check them against the Gospel and the words of Jesus.

SACRED THINGS

UPON COMPLETION OF THE WALL and assigning guards to be gatekeepers, Nehemiah returned to King Artaxerxes. In the time that he was away, the people violated the sacred things of the temple, the Sabbath, and marriage. Upon his return to Jerusalem, Nehemiah reacted to the situation.

> "And it grieved me bitterly; therefore I threw all the household goods of Tobiah out of the room" (Neh. 13:8).

Tobiah had been living in one of the storehouses of the temple. The next thing Nehemiah realized is that the people were working and buying and selling goods on the Sabbath. So, Nehemiah commanded the gates to be shut on the Sabbath.

> "Now the merchants and sellers of all kinds of wares lodged outside Jerusalem once or twice. Then I warned them, and said to them, 'Why do you spend the night around the wall? If you do *so* again, I will lay hands on you!' From that time on they came no *more* on the Sabbath" (Neh. 13:20-21).

He then saw that his people had married foreign women and were learning foreign languages.

> "So I contended with them and cursed them, struck some of them and pulled out their hair, and made them swear by God, *saying,* 'You shall not give your daughters as wives to their sons, nor take their daughters for your sons or yourselves'" (Neh. 13:25).

A lot of us think Nehemiah's behavior is not Christlike. But look at how Jesus reacted to the merchants in the temple:

> "Then Jesus went into the temple of God and drove out all those who bought and sold in the temple, and overturned the tables of the money changers and the seats of those who sold doves" (Matt. 21:12).

EYE-OPENING

WE HEAR PEOPLE TALK ABOUT having eye-opening experiences in which they obtain a better understanding of someone or something. The problem is that we think our eyes are what guide us. This is the way the serpent tricked Eve in the garden.

> "For God knows that in the day you eat of it your eyes will be opened, and you will be like God, knowing good and evil" (Gen. 3:5).

More often than not, our eyes are what make us wander off-course. Seeing is believing is our attitude. Jesus said:

> "The lamp of the body is the eye. If therefore your eye is good, your whole body will be full of light. But if your eye is bad, your whole body will be full of darkness. If therefore the light that is in you is darkness, how great *is* that darkness!" (Matt. 6:22-23).

The truth is that God is the only One Who can make our eyes open. Jesus opened the eyes of the blind as Isaiah had prophesied.

> "Then the eyes of the blind shall be opened, And the ears of the deaf shall be unstopped" (Isa. 35:5).

Jesus did not just heal the physically blind; more importantly, He also healed those who were blind in spirit and heart. He continues to do this even today. As He opens our eyes, He gives us a new lens with which to see the world around us. Love and compassion should flow from us as our eyes are being opened.

BUILDING GALLOWS

BE CAREFUL OF JUDGING OTHERS or attempting to persecute them. God is always watching. Haman is a perfect example of this. He was a powerful man in the kingdom of King Ahasuerus.

> "After these things King Ahasuerus promoted Haman, the son of Hammedatha the Agagite, and advanced him and set his seat above all the princes who were with him" (Esth. 3:1).

Haman had it in his heart to kill Mordecai and the Jews. Haman set out to build a fifty-foot gallow on which to hang Mordecai. He built it in front of his own house. Esther fasted and prayed for God's direction in order to save Mordecai and the Jewish people from the wrath of Haman. Haman's plan turned around on him, though, and the king ordered him to be hung on the very gallows he had built. In addition, later on, Haman's ten sons were all hung on the same gallows. The Jews were set free from persecution.

> "The Jews had light and gladness, joy and honor" (Esth. 8:16).

Pursue God, and allow Him to direct your path, and you will be filled with these things. Do not go about building gallows.

> "Judge not, that you not be judged. For with what judgment you judge, you will be judged; and with the measure you use; it will be measured back to you" (Matt. 7:1-2).

REMEDY FOR GRIEF

IN THE LIFE OF A Christian, there is a great remedy for grief or anxiety. We typically don't engage in this right away, but we should. The remedy is worship.

When Job received the news that his sons and daughters had all died, Scripture says:

> "Then Job arose, tore his robe, and shaved his head;
> and he fell to the ground and worshiped" (Job 1:20).

Job grieved violently, but then he turned to God and did the one thing that is needed. He worshipped. In spite of the circumstances, Job did not lose sight of the fact that God is good!

Whatever may be burdening you can be lifted from you when you make the choice to take your eyes off of yourself and place them on God. In turn, you will be filled with His presence. One of the reasons we were created was to worship Him. When we worship wholeheartedly, He will rise up inside of us, and we get to experience His glory.

TRUST

WHAT DOES IT MEAN TO trust? In this world, we only acquire the trust of someone through proving that we are worthy of trust. As Christians, we are called to trust God through faith. As we step out in faith, our trust in God is strengthened. In spite of the circumstances, we come to trust that God is in control. This trust produces an irrational peace that speaks of God louder than any of our words ever will. Are you resting in His peace or are you struggling with your flesh?

Job is a good example of someone who struggled but endured by trusting God. In his darkest hour, he said, "Why do I take my flesh in my teeth, And put my life in my hands? Though He slay me, yet will I trust Him" (Job 13:14-15).

In spite of the devastating circumstances he found himself in, Job declared his trust in God.

Jesus is the only One Who was slain by the Father. His death on the cross gives us the right to live and be righteous before the Father. Jesus declares:

> "All things have been delivered to Me by My Father, and no one knows the Son except the Father. Nor does anyone know the Father except the Son, and *the one* to whom the Son wills to reveal *Him*" (Matt. 11:27).

We need to entrust our lives to Jesus if we want to receive the revelation of the Father.

THE COMFORTER

WHEN JOB'S FRIENDS CAME TO comfort him, Job found himself speaking out against them.

> "I have heard many such things; miserable comforters *are* you all! Shall words of wind have an end? Or what provokes you that you answer? I also could speak as you *do*, If your soul were in my soul's place. I could heap up words against you, And shake my head at you; *But* I would strengthen you with my mouth, And the comfort of my lips would relieve *your grief*" (Job 16:2-5).

Job's friends were not speaking from God; they were speaking from their own understanding. This caused Job additional grief instead of relieving the immense grief he already had.

We need to be careful when we come into contact with brothers and sisters who are going through trials and tribulations. Jesus left us His Comforter or Helper in order that we might minister to one another, not judge each other.

> "But the Helper, the Holy Spirit, whom the Father will send in My name, He will teach you all things, and bring to remembrance all things that I said to you. Peace I leave with you, My peace I give to you; not as the world gives do I give to you. Let not your heart be troubled, neither let it be afraid" (Jn. 14:26-27).

We have been given this Comforter, or Helper, to remember the teachings of Jesus and attain peace. When a brother or sister is going through a trial, our call is not to judge, but to love and restore peace. We are a people who should learn to relieve grief, not create more. Be careful what you say when you come into contact with a grieving brother or sister.

FRUIT VS. CHAFF

THE PSALMIST COMPARES THE RIGHTEOUS to the ungodly in the first Psalm. The righteous man delights in the law of the Lord. He is compared to a tree by the water. He brings forth fruit.

> "Blessed *is* the man who trusts in the LORD, And whose hope is the LORD. For he shall be like a tree planted by the waters, Which spreads out its roots by the river, And will not fear when heat comes; But it's leaf will be green, And will not be anxious in the year of drought, Nor will cease from yielding fruit" (Jer. 17:7-8).

The water is the Word of God. The living water is Jesus. The ungodly are compared to chaff. Chaff are husks of corn. Corn is grown in huge quantities. Many are the husks of corn, but few are the trees.

> "Because narrow *is* the gate and difficult *is* the way which leads to life, and there are few who find it" (Matt. 7:14).

Chaff is also defined as "worthless matter."

As you look at your life, have you become chaff, along with the multitude of people; or are you a strong tree, grounded in the Word of God and the teachings of the Living Word—Jesus.

REJOICE IN YOUR SALVATION

JOYLESSNESS COMES FROM A CONCENTRATION on this fleshly life and the pursuits of selfish ambition. It is easy to lose sight of our salvation and become consumed by the cares of this world. If you find that the joy of your salvation has subsided, check to see if you have lost sight of God.

> "Have mercy on me, O LORD! Consider my trouble from those who hate me, You who lift me up from the gates of death, That I may tell of all Your praise. In the gates of the daughter of Zion. I will rejoice in Your salvation" (Psa. 9:13-14).

Our joy and gladness come from God's salvation only. This is why we need to keep our salvation at the forefront of our minds. When we lose sight of the gift of salvation, we become ungrateful and cease rejoicing.

A PERFECT WAY

PERFECTION ASIDE FROM GOD DOES not exist. Many may think that they have achieved perfection in one area or another; but when put under the light of the Almighty, the tiniest imperfections become visible. There is only One Who is perfect—God. He lays out the way before us. He delivers us from darkness, so that we can have faith.

> "He sent from above, He took me; He drew me out of many waters" (Psa. 18:16).

Once we begin to walk by faith, our imperfection becomes obvious, but God's perfection directs us.

> "*As for* God, His way *is* perfect; The word of the LORD is proven; He *is* a shield to all who trust in Him" (Psa. 18:30).

Many of us get confused as to what our part is. We get deceived into believing that we need to be the shield. Our role is to trust God and follow the way He lays out for us, having faith that is perfect beyond any measure of man.

PATIENCE

OUR WORLD IS FULL OF busybodies. We run around, trying to meet the demands the world places on us. We are occupied with so many ambitions to create security in a world that is not secure. It is because of our insecurities that we create false needs that then drive our lives. When someone tells us to wait, we get angry. Patience is a fruit of the Spirit. Scripture tells us, "Wait on the LORD; Be of good courage, And He shall strengthen your heart; Wait, I say, on the LORD!" (Psa. 27:14).

When you cease to wait on the Lord for His counsel, you get caught up in your own insecurities and worldly concerns. This, in turn, breeds impatience. Impatience robs you of peace. The psalmist, David, tells us that when we wait on the Lord, He strengthens our heart. A strong heart can endure many trials. A strong heart is not defeated by evil. A strong heart is my desire. I pray I learn to wait patiently on God.

RICHES AND LIGHT

THERE IS SOMETHING WRONG WITH our inner being. We see need. We see poverty. We see hurt. But our own needs cry louder to us than those of the less-fortunate. We turn away from those who ask for our help. Our hunger for comfort, possessions, and security consumes us. We think that God doesn't care about our needs, yet what we think we need is not at all what we really need.

> "Certainly every man at his best state *is* but vapor. *Selah* Surely every man walks about like a shadow; Surely they busy themselves in vain; He heaps up *riches*, And does not know who will gather them" (Psa. 39:5-6).

Jesus died on the cross so that we could be set free from bondage, yet we choose our bondage over the amazing love and freedom that Jesus gives us.

> "Let your light so shine before men, that they may see your good works and glorify your Father in heaven" (Matt. 5:16).

Our light is the love of Jesus, and darkness has no power over it. Light does not speak; it simply exists. Let Christ's love shine forth from you by letting go of this world and inviting Christ to be the center of your life.

ISRAEL AND US

"He *is* the Lord our God; His judgments *are* in all the
earth" (Psa. 105:7).

Like Israel, we fail to see that God is universal and controls everything. If you take the time to reflect back on your
journey with Jesus, you will see how He has orchestrated on
your behalf. Like Israel, it may have been through pain and
suffering. Like Joseph, we can be tested.

"He sent a man before them—Joseph—*who* was sold
as a slave. They hurt his feet with fetters, He was laid
in irons. Until the time that his word came to pass,
The word of the LORD tested him" (Psa. 105:17-19).

God may speak something to you that has not come to
pass yet; but stay faithful, and stand strong on the word that
He spoke, and you will be amazed. Like Joseph and Jesus, God
will set you free from the chains of affliction, and you will
rise from the oppression of your enemy.

PERSEVERE

THE ONLY THING THAT KEEPS God's Spirit alive in us is our perseverance. When things get dark, we have the choice to persevere or throw in the towel. Satan's goal is to get everyone to throw in the towel. We have to fight against the enemy.

When the Spirit of God is alive in us, it produces works. First, it produces the internal work in which our own hearts and minds are transformed. It will then overflow into those around us. God has given us a guidebook in the Bible and the Holy Spirit to guide us through life. Stop trying to build this earthly life of comfort, and start suffering for the message of Jesus.

> "Because you have kept My command to persevere, I also will keep you from the hour of trial which shall come upon the whole world, to test those who dwell on the earth" (Rev. 3:10).

We have a choice to persevere with Christ or suffer the trials of opposing Him.

ABUNDANT REDEMPTION

THE WORD *REDEEM* **MEANS "TO** free from captivity by payment of ransom." The redemption and mercy that is spoken of in Psalm 130 comes at a cost. The cost is death. Jesus Christ took our place on the cross so that we might be set free from the captivity of sin.

> "O Israel, hope in the Lord; For with the LORD *there is* mercy, And with Him *is* abundant redemption. And He shall redeem Israel From all his iniquities" (Psa. 130:7-8).

This redemption was first sent to the house of Israel and later extended to everyone. What Jesus did on the cross was so great, so powerful, so beyond our imagination, that it can redeem anyone from any sin.

> "Let the wicked forsake his way, and the unrighteous man his thoughts; Let him return to the LORD, and He will have mercy on him; And to our God, For He will abundantly pardon" (Isa. 55:7).

The person who has done wickedly has to give up their wickedness, and the unrighteous person has to let go of his or her thoughts. The problem is that we don't realize that everyone of us is wicked and unrighteous, and the only righteousness comes from Jesus' redemption in our lives.

> "For My thoughts *are* not your thoughts, Nor *are* your ways My ways," says the LORD" (Isa. 55:8).

The redemption process starts with a face-to-face encounter with our own wickedness and Jesus' love. The redemption process then continues throughout our lives.

PRAISE

WE PRAISE GOD BECAUSE HE deserves the glory. By praising Him, we guard our hearts from becoming prideful. When we praise wholeheartedly, all of our being is focused on God, and we become unaware of ourselves. Praise is given to God because He is the only Giver of lasting truth. It is when we cry out sincerely that we will receive from God.

> "In the day when I cried out, You answered me, *And* made me bold *with* strength in my soul" (Psa. 138:3).

It takes humility to cry out to God. God wants you to cry out to Him, and He wants to answer you.

> "Though the Lord *is* on high, Yet He regards the lowly; But the proud He knows from afar" (Psa. 138:6).

It is our pride that puts us at odds with our ever-present God. God wants to answer us, but He gave us free will to decide whether or not to humble ourselves and come to Him.

GOD'S OMNIPRESENCE

GOD IS EVERYWHERE, BUT HE is not in everything. The false message that is being taught today is that God can be found in everything or anything. Psalm 24 says, "The earth *is* the LORD's, and all its fullness, The world and those who dwell therein" (Psa. 24:1).

The truth is that we all belong to God, but not all of us follow Him. Paul said, "All things are lawful for me, but not all things are helpful; all things are lawful for me, but not all things edify" (1 Cor. 10:23).

God created the earth—and us—in perfection, but because of sin, we live in an imperfect world. When you accept Jesus into your life and receive the Holy Spirit, you realign yourself with God, and there is no place you can go that His Spirit will not be. David observed this in Psalm 139.

> "Where can I go from Your Spirit? Or where can I flee from Your presence? If I ascend into heaven, You *are* there; If I make my bed in hell, behold, You *are* there" (Psa. 139:7-8).

ABOMINATION

AN ABOMINATION IS SOMETHING THAT is repugnant to God. Solomon listed the things that are an abomination:

> "These six *things* the Lord hates, Yes seven *are* an abomination to Him: A proud look, a lying tongue, Hands that shed innocent blood, A heart that devises wicked plans, Feet that are swift in running to evil, A false witness *who* speaks lies, And one who sows discord among brethren" (Prov. 6:16-19).

A proud look is the one given when you think that you are superior to another. The proud person refuses to be humbled.

> "God resists the proud, But gives grace to the humble" (1 Pet. 5:5b).

A lying tongue and a false witness are also abominations. We are called to speak the truth in love. Speaking the truth without love will not be received. Remember, you will reap what you sow. If you sow the truth without love, that is what you will receive in return. If we didn't have discord or disagreement and quarrelling in the church, think of how powerful it would be. God hates discord because it destroys the brethren. It disconnects His Body. Solomon mentions the eyes, the tongue, the hands, the feet, and the heart. These are the parts of us that God has created for good, yet we choose to be instruments of the enemy. God loves peace and love. He will resist things that are in opposition to it. Are your eyes, tongue, hands, feet, and heart in submission to God? Humble yourself before Him, and He will lift you up.

DROSS

THE PROCESS OF REFINEMENT IS something we choose to endure or shrink away from. There is pain involved in refinement, but the outcome is a great one. When we speak out the things of God, He shows us His glory. When we surrender our lives, He begins to refine us. He needs to remove the dross from our lives in order to uncover the precious metal He has placed in us.

> "Take away the dross from silver, And it will go to the silversmith *for* jewelry" (Prov. 25:4).

A silversmith is one who makes, repairs, or sells articles made of silver. God created man; Jesus repaired man; and the Holy Spirit removes the dross in our lives.

> "But in a great house there are not only vessels of gold and silver, but also of wood and clay, some for honor and some for dishonor. Therefore if anyone cleanses himself from the latter, he will be a vessel for honor, sanctified and useful for the Master, prepared for every good work" (2 Tim. 2:20-21).

> Remember Daniel's interpretation of King Nebuchadnezzar's dream (Dan. 2:31-45)?

*Additional Dross verses for study: Psalm 119:119, Proverbs 26:23, Isaiah 1:22,25, Ezekiel 22:18-19

MY SHIELD

THE LORD IS MY ONLY Protection in this broken world. He guards me from all the things of this world that have power to devour me. When He speaks, my heart is made alive; and when He is silent, I know He is still there. Breaking down all my walls, He has reached me. I trust Him because I have seen that He is good.

> "Every word of God *is* pure; He *is* a shield to those who put their trust in Him. Do not add to His words, Lest He rebuke you, and you be found a liar" (Prov. 30:5-6).

Are His words not good enough for us? Did Jesus not say it clearly enough?

> "'... You shall love the LORD your God with all your heart, with all your soul, and with all your mind.' This is *the* first and great commandment. And the second *is* like it: 'You shall love your neighbor as yourself.' On these two commandments hang all the Law and the Prophets" (Matt. 22:37-40).

I give it all up to You, God!

COMPANION

SOLOMON WRITES MAINLY ABOUT THE vanity of life in Ecclesiastes. Until chapter four, we don't hear anything positive in Solomon's reflections. He then expresses the benefits of having a companion.

> Two *are* better than one, Because they have a good reward for their labor. For if they fall, one will lift up his companion. But woe to him *who is* alone when he falls, For *he has* no one to help him up. Again, if two lie down together, they will keep warm; But how can one be warm *alone*? Though one may be overpowered by another, two can withstand him. And a threefold cord is not quickly broken (Eccl. 4:9-12).

The devil seeks whom he may devour, and those of us with a lone wolf complex need to have this mindset removed from us. This idea that it's just you and God alone comes from your enemy. Jesus sent the disciples out, saying, "Behold, I send you out as sheep in the midst of wolves. Therefore be wise as serpents and harmless as doves" (Matt. 10:16).

After the twelve, Jesus appoints an additional seventy. He sent them two by two into every city and place where He Himself was about to go.

WISDOM

WORLDLY WISDOM IS IN OPPOSITION to godly wisdom. The wisdom of this world seeks to benefit only you, and wisdom from God will benefit Him and others. We will, however, be granted peace in pursuing His wisdom for our lives. How great is it when you discover something hidden about God. Solomon said, "A man's wisdom makes his face shine, And the sternness of his face is changed" (Eccl. 8:1b).

Let us desire His mind and not our own. When we seek the things of His kingdom, our needs will be met. This means that it is not our desires that are met, but our needs. Discerning between what is a personal want and what is God's will is wisdom.

SEAL OF LOVE

LOVE IS THE MOST POWERFUL emotion known to man. Through it, we can be changed or destroyed. My desire as a man is to conquer my woman with love. The world tells me to conquer women through power, money, and security, but love requires vulnerability, something most men see as weakness. Our love should be a fire that is unrelenting.

> "Set me as a seal upon your heart, As a seal upon your arm; For love *is as* strong as death, Jealousy *as* cruel as the grave; Its flames *are* flames of fire, A most vehement flame. Many waters cannot quench love; Nor can the floods drown it" (Songs of Sol. 8:6-7).

PILLARS TO GOD

IN THE OLD TESTAMENT, WE see many of God's people erecting pillars to God as a form of worship when a vow was taken. Jacob was the first person in the Bible to do this. He was traveling to Padan Aram to take a wife for himself when the Lord gave him a vision of a ladder that reached the heavens. On this ladder, the angels of God ascended and descended, and the Lord stood at the top. The Lord vowed to Jacob that He would give him land and bless him. When Jacob awoke, he placed the stone he had slept on as a pillar to God and anointed it with oil.

> "Then Jacob made a vow, saying, 'If God will be with me, and keep me in this way that I am going, and give me bread to eat and clothing to put on, so that I come back to my father's house in peace, then the LORD shall be my God. And this stone which I have set as a pillar shall be God's house, and of all that You give me I will surely give a tenth to You'" (Gen. 28:20-22).

This was the origin of the tithe. It is the way Jacob acknowledged God's blessing. Moses then erected twelve pillars at the base of Mount Sinai alongside the altar (Exodus 24). The same term for pillar is used for pagan religious practices. In Exodus 23:24, God commanded the Israelites to destroy the sacred pillars of the pagans they will conquer.

> "In that day there will be an altar to the LORD in the midst of the land of Egypt, and a pillar to the LORD at its border" (Isa. 19:19).

RYAN PHILLIPS 111

The angel of the Lord appeared to Joseph in a dream and warned him to take Jesus to Egypt. Jesus is the pillar to God. He is Jacob's ladder. When tearing down pillars, make sure that they are pagan pillars and not ones God has anointed.

> "I saw still another mighty angel coming down from heaven, clothed with a cloud. And a rainbow *was* on his head, his face *was* like the sun, and his feet like pillars of fire" (Rev. 10:1).

OUT OF EGYPT

GOD BROUGHT THE ISRAELITES OUT of their bondage from Egypt. He was gracious to them and did not place them in battle immediately.

> "Then it came to pass, when Pharoah had let the people go, that God did not lead them *by* way of the land of the Philistines, although that *was* near; for God said, 'Lest perhaps the people change their minds when they see war, and return to Egypt'" (Exod. 13:17).

God does not launch us into spiritual warfare when we first get saved and brought out of bondage. He allows us to develop a measure of faith first. He knows that we don't have the strength of mind and heart to endure. God is clearly guiding every moment because our faith is weak. He did the same with Israel.

> "And the LORD went before them by day in a pillar of cloud to lead the way, and by night in a pillar of fire to give them light, so as to go by day and night. He did not take away the pillar of cloud by day or the pillar of fire by night *from* before the people" (Exod. 13:21-22).

In the beginning of our walk with God, our faith is so weak that if we experience trial, we would turn back. God does not give us more than we can handle. If you endure, you will be granted a seat on Christ's throne.

> "Because you have kept My command to persevere, I also will keep you from the hour of trial which shall come upon the whole world, to test those who dwell on earth" (Rev. 3:10).

TAKING ROOT DOWNWARD

THROUGHOUT SCRIPTURE, WE SEE GOD exalting the lowly. He takes the outcast, the downtrodden, those deemed insignificant, and lifts them up to display His glory and power. God always wants us to humble ourselves because in doing so, we actually receive the things the Holy Spirit longs for in us. When Isaiah spoke the words of the Lord to Hezekiah, he said, "And the remnant who have escaped of the house of Judah Shall again take root downward, And bear fruit upward" (Isa. 37:31).

"John the Baptist understood this mystery when he declared, 'He must increase, but I *must* decrease'" (Jn. 3:30).

"Jesus later explained to Andrew and Philip, 'Most assuredly, I say to you, unless a grain of wheat falls into the ground and dies, it remains alone; but if it dies, it produces much grain'" (Jn. 12:24).

Part of being a Christian is humbling yourself. It's dying to your sinful nature in both your flesh and your mind. We need to be a people broken over our sin. Peter wrote, "God resists the proud, But gives grace to the humble. Therefore humble yourselves under the mighty hand of God, that He may exalt you in due time" (1 Pet. 5:5b-6).

A death to self is needed in order for a person to take root downward and bear fruit (love, joy, peace, etc.).

MY HANDS AND HIS HANDS

IN THE BEGINNING, GOD FORMED man out of the dust of the earth.

> "And the Lord God formed man *of* the dust of the ground, and breathed into his nostrils the breath of life; and man became a living being" (Gen. 2:7).

Since then, mankind has been using their hands to create and destroy. The sad part is a lot of people end up in bondage to things made by man. People strive their whole lives to preserve and maintain a standard of living they believe they need. In the end, this is the truth:

> "Then the dust will return to the earth as it was, And the spirit will return to God who gave it" (Eccl. 12:7).

We tend to think the people in the Old Testament, who worshipped carved images, were not that smart; but we do the exact same thing. Our carved images have gotten more sophisticated, but the human heart remains the same. Will you use your hands to build for His kingdom or yours?

> "And: You, LORD, in the beginning laid the foundation of the earth, And the heavens are the work of Your hands" (Heb. 1:10).

Ask the Holy Spirit to show you what your hands are created to do. He has placed great power in our hands.

SILENT SUFFERING

IN OUR FLESH, THERE IS a nature of avoiding suffering at all costs. When we do have to endure suffering, we tend to complain about it. We often believe that this couldn't be God's will. Our Lord and Savior, Jesus, suffered in silence. Isaiah foretold of this.

> "He was oppressed and He was afflicted, Yet He opened not His mouth; He was led as a lamb to the slaughter, And as a sheep before its shearers is silent, So He opened not His mouth" (Isa. 53:7).

What humble confidence to face crucifixion without uttering a word. And then to break the silence, He utters words of forgiveness.

> "Then Jesus said, 'Father, forgive them, for they do not know not what they do'" (Lk. 23:34).

What kind of love is this? After suffering the most intense pain a man can feel, Jesus asked that forgiveness be extended to those who had inflicted this pain upon Him. This is unheard of in human history. The Divine must have dumbfounded those who heard these words coming from Jesus. This is the kind of love the world needs. This is pure love. A willingness to show through actions, not words, the love of God is what silent suffering is all about. Silent suffering can produce in you a power uncommon in this world.

SWITCHING THE CURSE

THE CURSE PLACED ON MAN was that he would have to work hard for everything he needs and would face adversity throughout his life. God said:

> Cursed *is* the ground for your sake; In toil you shall eat *of* it All the days of your life. Both thorns and thistles it shall bring forth for you, And you shall eat the herb of the field. In the sweat of your face you shall eat bread Till you return to the ground, For out of it you were taken; For dust you *are*, and to dust you shall return" (Gen. 3:17b-19).

Jesus then switched the curse on the cross and blessed those who believe in Him. He is the Living Water, the One my soul longs for.

> "Ho! Everyone who thirsts, Come to the waters; And you who have no money, Come, buy and eat. Yes, come, buy wine and milk Without money and without price. Why do you spend money for *what is* not bread, And your wages for *what* does not satisfy?" (Isa. 55:1-2).

I think that if I save enough, I can change the curse; but that is never going to happen. Jesus wants you to come to Him. He wants you to rely on Him. He has lifted the curse, but we still live as if we are under it. Do you not see what He has done? He has changed you and me. We are in this world, but not of it. He desires to fill you up with His Spirit so that you can start living the Good News.

THE SPIRIT GIVING GLORY

THE SPIRIT OF THE LORD God was upon Jesus. Jesus was sent with Good News for the poor, the brokenhearted, and the imprisoned. The Spirit's purpose is clearly stated:

> "To console those who mourn in Zion, To give them beauty for ashes, The oil of joy for mourning, The garment of praise for the spirit of heaviness; That they may be called trees of righteousness, The planting of the LORD, that He may be glorified" (Isa. 61:3).

There is nothing worthy in my flesh, but God has planted a seed inside of me. The Spirit of God dwells inside of me. The Spirit comforts me and leads me into righteousness. When I receive the Spirit, the ashes of my life are turned into beauty and the mourning into joy; and the heaviness of my circumstances is lifted. I don't always experience this because it is a choice. There is a battle going on. Our purpose is not to be perfect in our flesh or to bring glory to ourselves, but to bring glory to God through surrender and faith.

> "Likewise the Spirit also helps in our weaknesses. For we do not know what we should pray for as we ought, but the Spirit Himself makes intercession for us with groanings which cannot be uttered" (Rom. 8:26).

In Mark nine, the father of a demon-possessed son asks Jesus to have compassion on him. "Jesus said to him, 'If you can believe, all things *are* possible to him who believes.' Immediately, the father of the child cried out and said with tears, 'Lord I believe; help my unbelief" (Mk. 9:23-24).

What a simple, true, and powerful prayer. Jesus healed the son. The flesh battled against the Spirit, and the Spirit gave glory to God.

HIS AGONY AND TEARS

WE ALL EXPERIENCE THE PAIN of agony at certain depths. What we do with our agony is what reveals our character. Do you soak in your misery or become embittered and angry? Jesus wept, but He did it without bitterness in his heart. He felt the deepest depths of human agony; He wept over Jerusalem.

> "Now as He drew near, He saw the city and wept over it, saying, 'If you had known, even you, especially in this your day, the things *that make* for your peace! But now they are hidden from your eyes" (Lk. 19:41-42).

Jesus's agony is that people cannot see how much He loves them, how much He desires for all of us to enter into His peace. Is your life falling in line with Jesus so that you shed tears for those who don't know Him? He gives us a new heart that experiences agony and pain over the sin in and around us. Have you ever wept over your condition, your neighbor, your town, your city, your nation, the world? Let us not become numb to the brokenness in and around us. It is never too late to stop and draw near to Jesus. He paid the price for your freedom.

CLINGING TO HIM

I CANNOT CLING TO JESUS and expect to not be broken and restored. As I cling to Jesus, He starts to chip away at my pride and selfishness. His Spirit comforts me; His Word encourages me; and the mystery drives me to know Him more. Letting go of this world can be hard at first; but when you experience God and His love, it is so complete, that nothing else is needed. In Jeremiah thirteen, God speaks to Jeremiah about Israel.

> Thus says the LORD: "In this manner I will ruin the pride of Judah and the great pride of Jerusalem. This evil people, who refuse to hear My words, who follow the dictates of their hearts, and walk after other gods to serve them and worship them, shall be like this sash which is profitable for nothing. For as the sash clings to the waist of a man, so I have caused the whole house of Israel and the whole house of Judah to cling to Me," says the LORD, "that they may become My people, for renown, for praise, and for glory; but they would not hear" (Jer. 13:9-11).

Am I clinging to Him, or have I ignored His voice?

For more information about
Ryan Phillips
&
Awakenings
please visit:

ryan@renewoutreach.org
www.ywamkona.org/donate/missionary/?id=6532
www.facebook.com/ryan.phillips.104418

For more information about
AMBASSADOR INTERNATIONAL
please visit:

www.ambassador-international.com
@AmbassadorIntl
www.facebook.com/AmbassadorIntl

*If you enjoyed this book, please consider leaving us a review on
Amazon, Goodreads, or our website.*

www.ingramcontent.com/pod-product-compliance
Lightning Source LLC
La Vergne TN
LVHW051419080426

835508LV00022B/3157